Praise for
Mapping the Psyche Volume 3: Kairos - The Astrology of Time

This lovely book embodies part 3 of Mapping the Psyche, and is a transcript of a course which brings students onward, from the study of an apparently static birth chart, into the ever moving universe. As students of Clare Martin, and readers of her two previous books, will recognise, Book 3, covering transits, returns, progressions and directions, is once again both immediately accessible and profound. It leads seamlessly from personal contributions from individual students, to philosophical discussion; to precise astronomical explanation and calculation; and to illuminating references to the historic roots of present day astrology.

As befits a course taught for the Centre of Psychological Astrology, the approach is "psychological", but equally respects the traditional skills in calculation of pre-computerised astrology, and the work of past masters in the astrological and psychological worlds. The title of Book 3 however is "Kairos" defined not as chronological time, but "time in between" – "the propitious moment for the performance of an action or the coming into being of a new state" and the recognition of the existence of such moments is the core theme of the book, in both a practical and philosophical sense. The understanding students need to acquire here of the tools of transits, progressions and directions is succinctly presented, as Clare directs her students to review their personal concerns in the light of the story told by placements in their charts at "that" moment in time.

A clear understanding of the process provides the reader with an opportunity to consciously align their lives with the movements of the heavens – to "do gladly that which I must do." In this way, the book offers not only a crystal clear exposition of astrological mechanics, but a genuine "map" for students to follow. It also excels as an invaluable reference source for experienced astrologers to cherish.

Teresa Early, Dip.Psych.Astrol

Mapping the Psyche

An Introduction to
Psychological Astrology

Volume 3: Kairos – The Astrology of Time

Clare Martin

The Wessex Astrologer

Published in 2015 by
The Wessex Astrologer Ltd,
4A Woodside Road
Bournemouth
BH5 2AZ
www.wessexastrologer.com

© Clare Martin 2015

Clare Martin asserts the moral right to be recognised as
the author of this work.

Cover Design by Jonathan Taylor
Cover picture, *Kairos*, from a fresco painted by Francesco Salviati
between 1552-1554, at the Palazzo Ricci Sacchetti in Rome

A catalogue record for this book is available at The British Library

ISBN 9781910531136

No part of this book may be reproduced or used in any form or by any
means without the written permission of the publisher.
A reviewer may quote brief passages.

CONTENTS

Time
    Lesson One   Introduction to Time   1
    Lesson Two   The Nature of Cycles   17
                               Retrograde Motion   28

Transits
    Lesson Three   Introduction to Transits   32
    Lesson Four   Transits of the Outer Planets   44
    Lesson Five   Transits of Saturn, Jupiter and Mars   68
                               and the Inner Planets
    Lesson Six   Planetary Returns   96
    Lesson Seven   Moon Cycles, Nodes and Eclipses   118
    Lesson Eight   Transits Case Study –   128
                               Dante Gabriel Rossetti

Progressions
    Lesson Nine   Secondary Progressions   148
                               Case Study – Dante Gabriel Rossetti   173

Solar Art Directions
    Lesson Ten   Solar Arc Directions   180
                               Case Study – Dante Gabriel Rossetti   186

Selected Bibliography   197

LESSON 1

An Introduction to Time

Clare: A very warm welcome back to everyone – it's good to see you all again. Our task this term is to consolidate what we have already learned and to embark on the study of astrological timing techniques.

In a sense, there is nothing fundamentally new for us to grasp this term – the birth chart will remain central and we will be working with the same planets, signs, houses and aspects, as before. But by bringing time into the equation, we are expanding our astrology from the static, fixed pattern of the natal chart into a dynamic story which unfolds in time.

The more examples you can bring to class for us to look at, the better. This is where our practical apprenticeship begins, and there is no substitute for actual experience. At the same time, it would be a good idea to continue to read as much as you can about Jung's ideas and concepts so that our astrological and psychological knowledge grow side by side.

We are going to spend this term exploring the major astrological forecasting techniques: transits, returns, progressions and directions. Psychologically, all these techniques represent opportunities for the development of consciousness.

But first of all, let's take some time to consider the philosophical implications of forecasting in astrology, which always bring up the perennial and vexed question of the relationship between fate and free will and the understandable distaste for, or fear of, astrology when it is assumed to be a fated system.

Audience: I find this is the biggest problem when I tell people I'm studying astrology. Generally they think it is scary and dangerous because it's about fate. And I think this is why people are so quick to judge astrology, even if they know nothing about it.

Clare: That's right, which is why we need to grasp this particular nettle right at the start.

Fate and Free Will

In Greek mythology, the three Fates were known as the Moirae, or 'apportioners', since they controlled the metaphorical thread of life from birth to death and beyond. They can be compared with the Norns, the three spinners of destiny in northern European mythology. The Fates are almost always depicted as old crones or hags, cold, remorseless and unfeeling. The three Moirae, or 'spinsters', were Clotho, Lachesis and Atropos. Clotho, the spinner, spun the thread of life from her distaff onto her spindle. Lachesis, the 'alotter', measured the thread of life with her rod, and Atropos, the 'inexorable' or 'inevitable', was the cutter of the thread of life, choosing the manner of a person's death.

The connection between astrology and fate is very ancient and we might even say that astrology itself evolved in response to the urge to understand the relationship between the cycles of the planets and an individual's or nation's fate.

Astrology with the Three Fates, 16th century, Arsenal Library, Paris.

In one sense it is absolutely true that the birth chart is our fate. It is our raw material – the inherent pattern we are born with, and stuck with, if you like. We are born with a specific north, south, east, west orientation as defined by the angles, and we are born with planets in certain signs and houses and in particular relationships to each other – and there is nothing we can do about that. We cannot trade in our cards and deal again – because the pattern has already been set at our birth. Indeed, we could even go as far as to say that nothing which is not on the birth chart as potential will ever come to pass.

Audience: That is a very strong statement to make.

Clare: Our birth charts are a reflection of the quality of the time and place at which we were born – and one way to think about this is in terms of frequency and resonance. Nothing outside our particular frequency and resonance can or will be experienced by the individual. In his book *The Challenge of Fate*, Thorwald Dethlefsen writes that, "in order to perceive something, a human being needs a corresponding vibration in themselves and it is this resonance which makes perception possible". Everything that lies outside our capacity to resonate cannot be perceived by us, and therefore does not exist for us. So we can say with some certainty, for example, that a person with Saturn in the fifth house, the house which rules gambling, is unlikely to win the lottery, since Saturn's function is to reward hard work and effort, not speculation.

This means that our experience of the external world and of other people is the most reliable source of information about ourselves, and this is one explanation of the phenomenon of synchronicity.

Audience: Can you define synchronicity for us?

Clare: This is a concept originally introduced by Jung, describing simultaneous occurrences which are meaningful to an individual, but causally unrelated. Synchronous events appear to reveal underlying patterns, or 'acausal connecting principles' which are always present but which we only occasionally experience consciously. For example, if we are thinking of buying a particular make of car, then we are likely to suddenly start seeing that make of car everywhere. If we become pregnant, then everywhere we go we will start seeing pregnant women. We have started to vibrate on those particular 'car' or 'pregnancy' frequencies, so we are accessing themes which are always there, in the background – like archetypes – but which we are not always conscious of.

The Moirae 16th century tapestry

Another point about fate is that from the moment of birth we can calculate with absolute precision the exact timing of all the transits, progressions and directions which will occur throughout our lives. They are all contained or enfolded within the birth chart as future events and they will happen anyway, whether we believe in fate or not. And whether we are astrologers or not. If this was not true, then astrological forecasting would not work.

So it is hardly surprising that forecasting plays such a major part in our art – and it is hard to think of any other discipline in which future developments are so clearly and accurately known. But of course it is not the events themselves which are of interest, but how we engage with them and what we do with them which is the challenge and purpose of our psychological approach to astrology.

Let's look at some dictionary definitions, to help us clarify what we are actually doing when we are engaged in astrological prediction and forecasting.

Prediction and Forecasting: The words prediction and forecasting are, to some extent, interchangeable. They are both defined as 'statements made about the future', with prediction being a more general term, and a forecast being more specific.

The dictionary tells us that a prediction is: "A statement or a claim that a particular event will occur in the future". The word (which comes from the Latin 'prae', meaning 'before' and 'dicere' meaning 'to say') means 'to say before'.

Well obviously we know from our ephemerides exactly where Saturn, for example, will be on the 15th July 2024. That's a prediction, isn't it? That's 'to say before.' We know it will be there, but can we predict how it will manifest or what that will mean to the individual? That's the interesting thing.

To forecast or foretell is "to predict in advance, to judge to be probable", such as a weather forecast, for example. Weather forecasting is "an attempt to predict the future tendency by examining and analysing the available data" – and we could equally apply this definition to astrological forecasting. In essence, there is no difference in method between weather forecasting, business and financial forecasting, and astrological forecasting.

The Three Moirae
Part of *A Golden Thread*, John Strudwick, 1885.

Prophecy is something else – "a prediction uttered under divine inspiration" or "knowledge of the future obtained from a divine source". So now divine agency is included, which means that our future will unfold as the gods have decreed. In ancient Greece the prophecies of the oracle were considered to be infallible. However cryptic the message, your fate would play itself according to the prophecy, no matter what you did to avoid it. The myth of Oedipus is a particularly well known example of this. So we can say that prophesies put us into a passive condition, subject to the whims of divine beings or forces.

The word '**destiny**' implies that there is a fixed, natural order to the universe and that our lives have purpose, however hidden that might be. Most of us believe in destiny, to the extent that we feel that our number 'comes up', or that an event was somehow 'meant to be' or that a particular bullet 'has our name on it'. There are many stories which tell of the futility of trying to out-manoeuvre our fate or destiny. Human beings are just as interested in their destiny now as they have always been, and this is, of course, why people are still fascinated and intrigued by astrology.

Entelechy: The word 'entelechy' is more organic, and gets closer to describing the quality of astrological and alchemical time. The word was originally coined by Aristotle and is a combination of the Greek words 'en', meaning 'in', 'telos', meaning the 'end', the 'purpose' or the 'goal', and 'ekhein', meaning 'to have' or 'to see'. It can be literally translated as 'having the end within itself' – or the process of something 'actively working to realise its potential' or its inherent essence. It is the vital force within any living organism which directs that organism towards self-fulfilment. So we could say that it is our inner nature which determines the shape of our lives.

Joseph Campbell observed that it is only in retrospect that what appeared at the time to be accidental and unrelated encounters and events in our lives can be seen to have been part of our entelechy:

> "One may find it difficult to resist the notion of the course of one's biography as comparable to that of a cleverly constructed novel, wondering who the author of the surprising plot can have been ..."[1]

And Jung suggested that:

> "The ego must be able to listen attentively and to give itself, without any further design or purpose, to that inner urge toward growth ..."[2]

Kairos: There is another very important word we need to consider, and I think it is essential that we grasp its meaning and use this in our work. The ancient Greeks had two words for time, 'chronos', which refers to chronological time, and 'kairos', which signifies a 'time in between' when something magical can happen. So chronos is quantitative, and kairos is qualitative.

Kairos is defined as "the opportune and decisive moment; the time when conditions are right for the accomplishment of a crucial action". It is "the propitious moment for the performance of an action or the coming into being of a new state".

Marie-Louise von Franz wrote that the alchemists knew about the importance of working with kairos. They knew that chemical processes only occurred at the astrologically right moment. If alchemists were working with silver, then the Moon, which is the planet of silver, had to be in the right position. And if alchemists were working with copper, then Venus, which is the planet of copper, had to be in a certain constellation.

One cannot just take those two metals and unite them, but must also consider and wait for the astrological constellation and pray to those planet gods and, if these things are also in order, then the chemical operation might work. Kairos means the astrologically right time, the time when things can turn out successfully. The alchemist is the man who must not only know the technique but must always consider these constellations.[3]

According to the ancient Greeks, kairos was the god of the 'fleeting moment' when time intersects with eternity, presenting a favourable opportunity to *oppose* the natural order of things. Such a moment must be grasped, otherwise it is gone and cannot be re-captured.

Kairos is "a passing instant when an opening appears which must be driven through with force if success is to be achieved".[4] And this is extremely exciting, because it exactly describes our alchemical approach as psychological astrologers. We need to take advantage of the kairos and to actively participate in and cooperate with the moment presented.

This understanding of kairos lies behind the famous motto 'Carpe Diem', and is linked with the wheel of fortune which continuously rotates, and was used by the poet and astronomer/astrologer Aratus to describe the eternal motion of the celestial spheres.[5] Here is a picture of the wheel of fortune in the famous medieval Burana Codex, in which the figures are labelled "Regno, Regnavi, Sum sine regno, Regnabo": I reign, I reigned, My reign is finished, I shall reign.

Wheel of Fortune
From *The Burana Codex*

It is really worth looking at these big questions, because our own assumptions about the nature of fate, destiny and time will inevitably affect our approach to astrological forecasting work. How fearful are we? Are we courageously and joyfully riding the wheel of fortune in our own lives, engaging actively with the dance of time, or are we afraid of it? If we are fearful or apprehensive, that fear and apprehension will automatically transmit itself to our clients and inhibit our ability to engage creatively with forecasting work.

The interesting question here is whether the universe is a living, breathing organism which actively responds to the quality of our engagement with it. This is something to keep in mind when we are looking at the whole subject of prediction and forecasting.

As human beings, we are meaning-seeking creatures, looking for patterns and models which will give shape to otherwise seemingly random events. It is the astrologer who breathes meaning into the horoscope, and to the extent that we carry the projection of the seer, sage, shaman, priest, witch or magician archetypes, we will be assumed to be in possession of some kind of enhanced, metaphysical or philosophical, level of understanding and knowledge.

The Wheel of Fortune
Edward Burne Jones

For this reason the astrologer has an equal potential to either heal or wound, and this is why we must examine our own assumptions and prejudices all the time and study our own charts all the time so that we can get out of our own way as much as possible and hold up the cleanest mirror to our clients that we are capable of. Astrology's greatest gift is its ability to help us see our own reflection in the cosmos, and the mirroring itself is fundamentally healing. But if we are fearful, either consciously or unconsciously, the mirror we hold up to our clients will be obscured, darkened and distorted.

We die with the same chart we were born with, so the question is what, if anything, has happened? Are we any more conscious by the time we die than we were when we were born? Have we used the kairos consciously in order to oppose the natural order of things? Have we lived our life or has life lived us? These are the questions, and the chart does not give us the answers. But I think the purpose of our psychological approach, coupled with Jung's conviction that the psyche has an inherent urge towards wholeness and integration, encourages us to jump onto the wheel of fortune, to grapple and engage fully with all the struggles and joys, and to live our lives to the full. Otherwise, as Gurdjieff said, the future will be exactly the same as the past – how could it be otherwise?

TIME AND SPACE

In astrology, time and space are fundamentally connected and in fact the birth chart itself is a map of the relationship between time and space. Roughly speaking, there are three ways of understanding how time unfolds through space – linear, cyclical and spiral.

Linear Time moves forwards in a straight line, so to speak. In linear time, yesterday preceded today and tomorrow will follow today, just as the 19th century preceded the 20th century and has now been succeeded by the 21st century, and so on. Everything in the physical world, such as our bodies, is subject to linear time, moving forwards in time from birth to death.

Cyclical Time

Astrological time is fundamentally cyclical, concerned with the unfolding of daily, monthly, yearly and planetary cycles. In astrological time, each cycle is symbolically identical and is interpreted in exactly the same way, no matter what its scale.

*Astrological Clock
Prague*

The ancient Greek philosophers were fascinated by the notion of great epochs of time, and many of these, such as Plato's Great Year, derive from mathematical symbolism. For Plato, the universe was a single living, rhythmic organism, subject to the two opposing principles of strife and love, and it was the tension between these two principles which created life itself. The number 36 was the key number of change, and the universe breathed in for 36,000 years, during which there was an increase of strife, and breathed out for 36,000 years, during which there was an increase of love, with each complete cycle being 72,000 years long. Like the Assyrians before him, Plato believed that the crisis or turning points in these cycles coincided with powerful conjunctions occurring on the Cancer/Capricorn axis. It was humanity's task to align and harmonise itself with these great rhythms, to help the universe to balance itself. So we could say that Plato's approach is identical to our own modern psychological approach.

Audience: This is such a beautiful, poetic way of looking at the universal patterns.

Clare: Yes, and here is Plato's equally poetic definition of time and the cosmic order, which you will find in the *Timeaus*:

> "The Creator resolved to have a moving image of eternity, and when he set in order the heaven, he made this image eternal but moving according to number, while eternity itself rests in unity; and this image we call time."

The astrologer Charles Harvey who, along with John Addey, made a tremendous contribution to the revival of our modern interest in astrological cycles and the harmonics of number, wrote: "The planetary cycles are the threads of eternity which weave the great tapestry of life in time", which I think is a beautiful image.

The next significant cycle down in scale is the 26,000 year cycle also known as the Great Year, which has an astronomical basis. We all know that the Earth's axis is tilted – by approximately 23½° – in relation to the Sun's path, the ecliptic, and it is this tilt which gives us our seasons and which is the basis of the tropical zodiac which we use in western astrology.

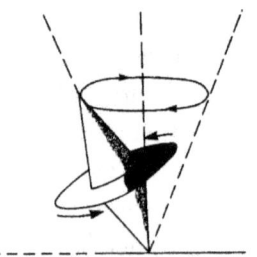

This tilt means that the poles of the Earth move around the poles of the ecliptic once every 26,000 years, in an action not unlike a gyroscope, and this phenomenon is know as the 'precession of the equinoxes'.

Our pole star – the star in the north which is 90° from the Earth's equator – is currently Polaris in the tail of the constellation of the Little Bear, Ursa Minor. But back in 3,000 BC the pole star was actually Thuban,

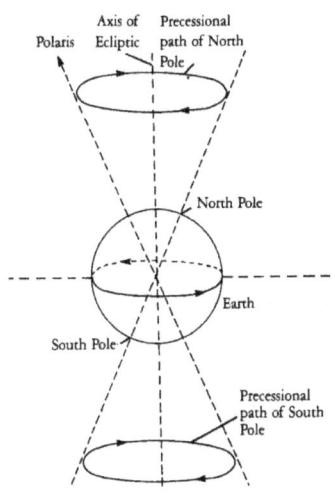

in the constellation of Draco, the great celestial dragon around which the axis of the world endlessly circles. Ancient buildings such as the Great Pyramid in Egypt were aligned to the north star at the time, and can therefore be accurately dated by astro-archeologists.

Dividing the Great Year by twelve will give us the great months, or twelve astrological ages, each of which lasts roughly 2000 years.

Audience: So is that the origin of the idea of the Age of Aquarius?

Clare: Exactly right. What is actually happening astronomically is that the Sun precesses or cuts the celestial equator very slightly earlier every spring equinox, as it crosses into the northern hemisphere. Every 72 years it precesses 1°, taking approximately 2,000 years for it to precess through a whole sign of 30° degrees. During the last 2,000 years this has occurred in the sign of Pisces.

Audience: So now we are entering the Age of Aquarius and leaving the age of Pisces behind?

Clare: Yes, that's right, so we are moving from a mutable cross to a fixed cross.

Audience: Can I ask what you mean by that?

Clare: Well, this is really a whole different subject, but we can say that the Age of Pisces included the other signs on the mutable cross. So for example, Pisces is balanced by its opposite sign of Virgo, which accurately describes the monastic life of spiritual devotion (Pisces) and practical service (Virgo) which was such a feature of the age. The Christian symbolism for this age is not only the sign of the fish but includes the important parable of the loaves of Virgo and the fish of

Pisces, not to mention the powerful cult of the Virgin, which has been such a feature of Catholicism. The Sagittarius-Gemini axis completes the mutable cross, giving us the three major religions of the book: the Torah, Bible and Talmud, and the age of exploration, from the Crusades to the discovery of new continents to the landing on the Moon. Those are the four mutable signs, and therefore the Age of Pisces has taken place on the mutable cross.

All cycles take a while to get established, it can take several hundred years in a 2,000-year cycle for the new themes to become well established following their first emergence. So we can say that the Aquarian Age is still in an embryonic stage, with the first stirrings occurring in the late 18th century around the discovery of Uranus in 1781, and the French, American and Scientific Revolutions, when utopian ideals for humanity such as equality and the brotherhood of man emerged alongside the development of the modern scientific method. And of course the sign of Aquarius is ruled by two planets which appear to be mutually exclusive, and it is the tendency of Saturn and Uranus to pull apart from each other, leading to increased fragmentation. The forces of change and stasis are in constant confrontation, but as we move into the Age of Aquarius, it seems that we are now collectively at the point when we must grapple with this whole issue, and recognise that all collectives, all groups and social structures have twin needs which do not need to be mutually exclusive – the need for stability and the need for adaptation and change.

Jung believed that the challenge of the Aquarian age is for human beings to take responsibility for integrating their inner opposites, both light and dark aspects, and he used the symbol of the anthropos – a cosmic image of wholeness – to illustrate this. So this is quite a challenge, but one to which his life work was devoted.

So we are in the collective process of shifting from the mutable cross to the fixed cross of the Age of Aquarius, which includes the signs Leo, Scorpio and Taurus. This means that we are going to have to grapple with questions of the Earth's resources in relation to our collective survival, and the role of the individual in the group, or the balancing of the heart and the head. So the fixed cross is not just about Aquarian themes but about the other signs on the fixed cross.

Audience: I don't suppose we can predict what's going to happen in the next 500 years?

Audience: Do we care? (Laughter)

Clare: The important point here is that, in addition to the drama of our personal lives, we are living at a time of immense transition during which the themes and values of the old age are dying and we are experiencing the painful birth of the next age. This puts our lives into perspective, helps us realise that we are part of something bigger, which I think is one of the most valuable gifts that astrology can give us.

Spiral Time

If we combine linear and cyclical time the result will be a spiral. Perhaps the biggest cycle we can hope to get our heads around is the 200 million year journey of the Sun around the centre of our galaxy, the Milky Way. The Sun, which is of course the centre of our solar system, is actually travelling at 200 miles a second and, if you can imagine the planets orbiting the Sun as it hurtles through space, then you will see an unfolding spiral.

And this is the most important idea I want to get over to you tonight, because it describes how we apply forecasting techniques in our astrological work.

Tad Mann has done some extremely interesting work on spiral time in his books *Life Time Astrology* and *The Divine Plot*, and the following diagrams are adapted from these books.

The first diagram (overleaf) gives us an interesting way to look at time and space as a three dimensional column, with each birth chart being a slice, or section, through this column, fixing the pattern for a whole lifetime, but also showing how time will continue to unfold after birth. This diagram tells us the exact positions of all the planets in the past as well as in the future. So each birth chart connects us to both the past and future.

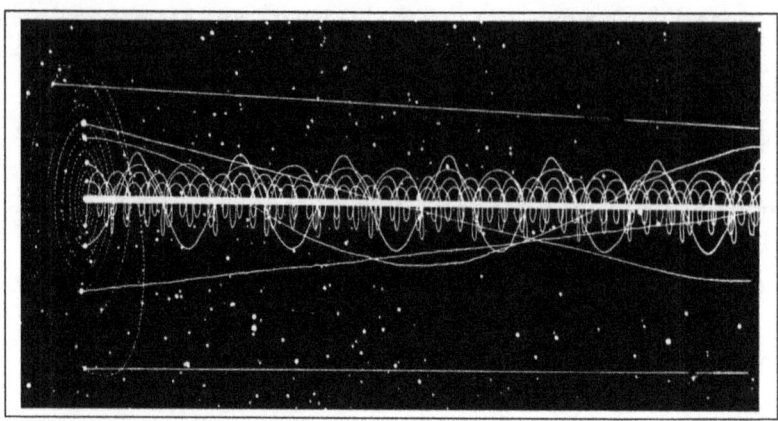

The small spirals close to the Sun's path represent the orbits of the inner planets Mercury, Venus, Earth and Mars, the medium size spirals represent the orbits of the planets Jupiter and Saturn, and the large spiral represents the orbits of the outer planets.

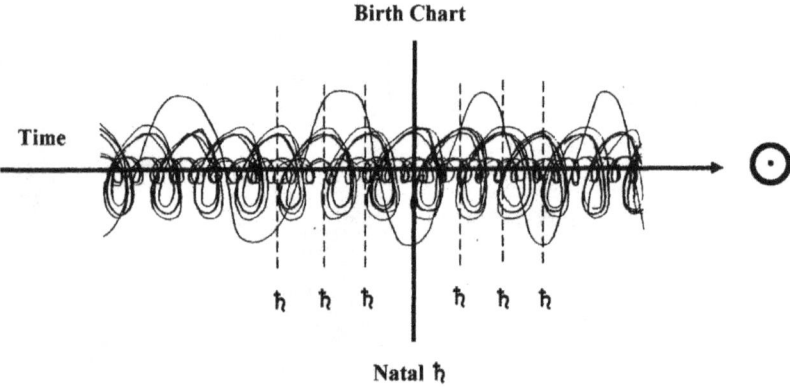

Using Saturn as an example, we know its exact position at birth, which means that we know exactly when it was and will be on this same position both before and after birth. This position can be extrapolated for thousands of years in either direction – although we are usually most concerned with its 29-year cycle during our lifetimes. The point is that when Saturn returns to its natal position 29 and 58 years after we were born – or before we were born, for that matter – it will have a particular resonance which we will respond to, since it reflects our core pattern, set at birth. In this way, we take our place in history and in the unfolding of time and, potentially, in the development of consciousness, to the extent that our approach is alchemical and we are working 'to perfect nature', to transform our lead into gold.

Audience: What about new planets which are discovered in our lifetime – will that change our knowledge?

Clare: Yes, the meaning of the word 'discover' is to reveal something which was previously 'covered' or unknown. When we work on historical charts we can see the outer planets playing a role in the lives of people even before they were discovered. The only difference is that there was no possibility of engaging with them consciously, since planets which are not yet known about 'out there' cannot be consciously realised 'in here'.

Audience: So you are saying that if we are aware and conscious of something, then we have some choice in the matter?

Clare: Exactly, and that is the purpose of our psychological approach. And if we are working with kairos, the forecasting techniques tell us the right time to act and then our astrology will actually make a difference – but it doesn't just make a difference for us personally – it makes a difference for the whole. One tiny particle of consciousness added to this time/space spiral is built into the system for all time. That is the alchemical approach, which is to perfect nature itself. And I think that is really important because our approach determines how we do our astrology and how we engage with the various forecasting techniques.

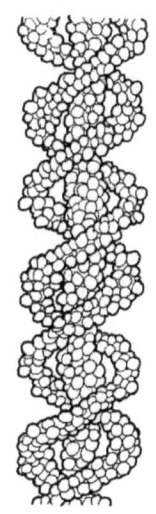

Audience: These spiral pictures remind me of the DNA helix.

Clare: Yes, and this is something Tad Mann has also pointed out. So the question is, could we actually be working on our personal and collective DNA? That would certainly be one way of looking at the alchemical

DNA Double Helix

process and at what we are doing with our psychological approach. Information is fed forwards from the past into the present, and even fed back to the present from the future.

Before we end this evening, it is worth giving some thought to the eternal realms and principles which are not caught up in the time/space spiral. As Ken Wilber writes: "Many cosmologies have a materialistic bias and prejudice: the physical cosmos is somehow supposed to be the most real dimension, and everything else is explained with ultimate reference to this material plane. But what a brutal approach that is!"[6] The spiritual and mystery traditions have always considered both the relative nature of time and the absolute nature of eternity, as in the following passage from the Bhagavad Gita:

> "In this world there are two orders of being: the perishable, separate creature and the changeless spirit."[7]

And Jung has made a similar differentiation:

> "The unconscious has no time. There is no trouble about time in the unconscious. Part of our psyche is not in time and not in space. They are only an illusion, time and space, and so in a certain part of our psyche time does not exist at all."[8]

So, although we will be studying time this term, it is worth remembering that the time/space spiral is only one aspect of our existence.

Notes
1. Joseph Campbell (1986), *The Inner Reaches of Outer Space: Metaphor as Myth and as Religion*, p.110.
2. C.G. Jung (Ed.), (1978) *Man and his Symbols*, Picador, Pan Press, p.163.
3. Marie-Louise von Franz, *Alchemy: An Introduction to the Symbolism and the Psychology* (1980), Inner City Books, p.44.
4. E. C. White (1987), *Kaironomia*, Cornell University Press, p.13
5. Aratus, *Phaenomena*, pp.227, 309.
6. Ken Wilber (1996), *A Brief History of Everything*, p.17.
7. The Bhagavad-Gita: 15:18-19, p.186.
8. C G Jung, *Collected Works* vol. 18, para. 684.

LESSON 2

The Nature of Cycles

Every cycle in nature and in astrology unfolds in the same way, no matter how large or small its scale. In each case, there is a birth, followed by a period of growth and expansion, a maturing and mellowing period, and then a gradual weakening and dying away in preparation for the next cycle. Charles Harvey writes that: "The different phases of any cycle represent the sequence of processes through which any idea passes in its total unfoldment."[1]

Whether we apply this principle to the daily cycle of the Sun, the monthly cycle of the Moon, the annual cycle of the zodiac, our own life cycle or even to historical epochs and civilisations, the pattern is the

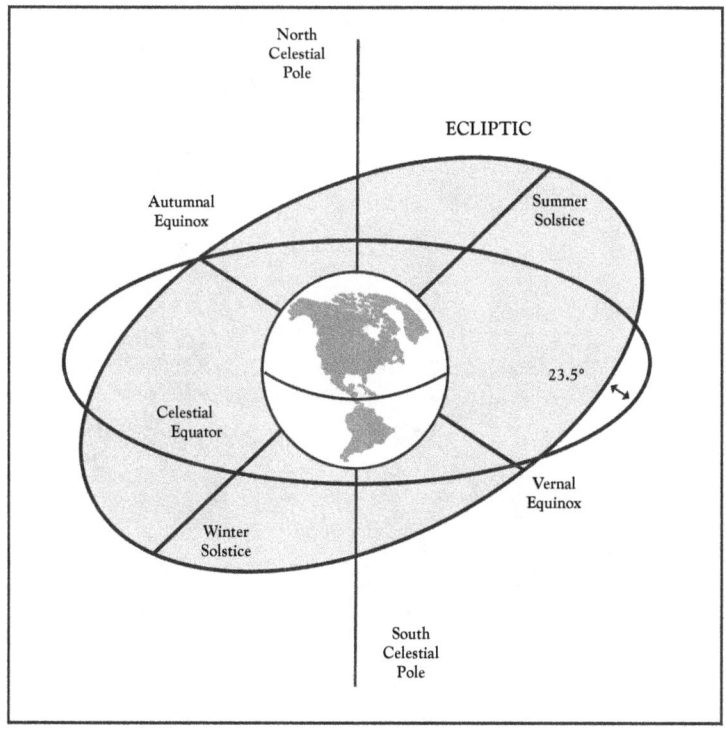

same. The point is that each cycle goes through the same developmental stages, no matter whether it is one day long or 2,000 years long.

Our tropical zodiac provides the basic template for the interpretation of all cycles in astrology. There are four major turning points in the tropical zodiac, marking the Sun's changing relationship with the Earth and defining the seasons in the northern hemisphere. These are the cardinal points, beginning at 0° Aries, the spring – or vernal – equinox, when the Sun crosses the celestial equator travelling north. The Sun grows in strength, reaching its maximum height at 0° Cancer, the point of the summer solstice, after which it begins its journey south, crossing

Agricultural tasks associated with Virgo/Libra time.
From the *Book of Hours*, Duc du Berry

the celestial equator once again at 0° Libra, the point of the autumn equinox. It reaches its furthest point south at 0° Capricorn, the winter solstice, at which point it begins to climb in the sky again. So the astrological signs of the tropical zodiac are absolutely connected to the seasons, to the agricultural year and to the traditional seasonal rituals.

Audience: How does this all work in the southern hemisphere, where the seasons are reversed?

Clare: That is a good question and difficult to answer. Our western tradition has evolved over thousands of years as a northern hemisphere system and was only imported to the southern hemisphere a few hundred years ago by indigenous European peoples. So, to the extent that it relates to the seasons in the northern hemisphere, the tropical zodiac is a displaced system. Sidereal astrology, however, which measures the positions of the planets against the stars and constellations, is not affected by the change in hemisphere.

All cycles in astrology begin symbolically at the point of the spring equinox, or 0° Aries, and unfold through the signs of the zodiac right the way through to Pisces, before beginning again at 0° Aries.

Every planetary pair has a conjunction point, which is symbolically related to the 0° Aries point. This is what Dane Rudhyar wrote about the cyclical relationship between two planets:

> "No aspect between two celestial bodies moving at different speeds – as they all do – can be truly understood unless it is considered as a particular phase of the cyclic process established by successive conjunctions of the two bodies. The actual meaning of the cyclic series of aspects, from conjunction to conjunction, depends on the character of the two related planets, but the *basic pattern* of all such cycles has the same abstract, or rather 'archetypal', character. If we understand the archetypal pattern of the cycle – that is, of any cycle of relationship between two interacting entities – we have in mind an instrument of universal validity."[2]

So let's have a closer look at the *basic pattern* of meaning which Dane Rudhyar applies to all cycles. Each cycle has two main phases, the waxing phase and the waning phase, each of which has a very different basic orientation and expression.

The **waxing** phase, from conjunction to opposition, from the spring to the autumn equinox and from the new to the full Moon is the evolutionary phase of the cycle, relating to the process of growth and development, moving towards the point of maximum expansion. The waxing phase is enthusiastic, outgoing and forward-looking, with an emphasis on exploration and growth. What Dane Rudhyar calls the 'seed idea' embedded in the conjunction will be actively developing and establishing itself in the world.

The **waning** Phase, from the opposition to conjunction, from the autumn to the spring equinox and from the full Moon back to the following new Moon, is the involutionary phase, which is more mature and philosophical. This is a phase of increasing reflectiveness, caution and withdrawal, with an emphasis on consolidation, passing on what has been learned, and sowing the seeds for the next cycle. Dane Rudhyar calls this the 'disseminating' half of the cycle, when what is harvested at the opposition is then distributed to the world.

This cycle applies both to single planets, which have their 'seed idea' embedded in the natal chart according to the sign and house they are in, and also to all planetary pairs, which have their 'seed idea' in the conjunction. In both cases, this point is symbolically placed at 0° Aries. The faster planet will move away from the slower planet and the meaning of the cycle will unfold sequentially from 0° Aries through each sign of the zodiac until the next conjunction.

Audience: Can you explain this a bit more please, Clare?

Clare: Yes, have a look at this diagram (on following page), which combines the growth cycle of plants with the monthly cycle of the Moon and annual cycle of the Sun, although the sequence of developmental stages can equally well be applied to every cycle in astrology.

All cycles begin symbolically at the 0° Aries point, and the entire potential and purpose, or 'entelechy' of the cycle, is contained in that seed moment of the conjunction. Dane Rudhyar used the life cycle of plants to describe this process, from the planting of the seed at the 0° Aries point, to germination in Taurus, to the first shoots in Gemini,

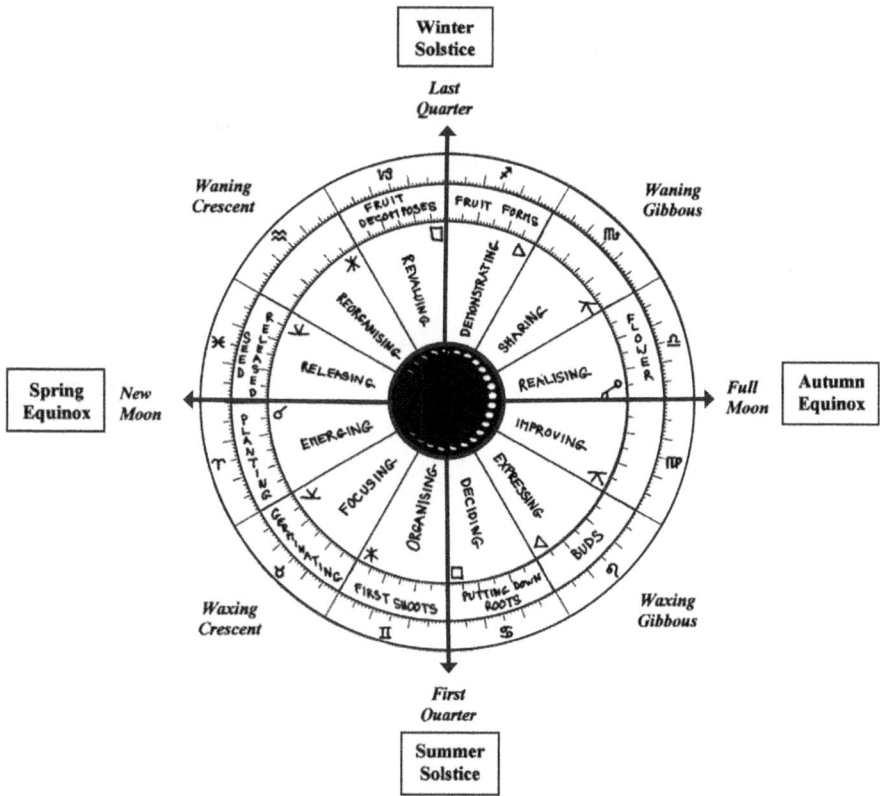

putting down roots in Cancer, to buds in Leo, culminating with the flower in Libra, at the opposition. During the waning phase, the fruit forms in Sagittarius, decomposes in Capricorn and finally the seed is released in Pisces for the next growth cycle. Every phase in the cycle has its essential part to play.

In every cycle there is a continuous organic movement, as one phase gradually turns into another, although there are four definite crises, or turning points in the cycle at the squares and opposition – occurring symbolically at 0° of the cardinal signs – and four more minor crisis points at the semi-squares and sesqui-quadrates – occurring symbolically at 15° of the fixed signs.

The four major turning points in the annual cycle occur at the equinoxes and solstices. The Sun enters Aries at the spring equinox and passes through the first three signs. This is "a period of instinctive, youthful, essentially unconscious and irrepressible activity", with the key words for Aries, Taurus and Gemini being *emerging*, *focusing* and *organising*. When the Sun enters Cancer at the summer solstice, the crisis of the square aspect demands the conscious establishment of the cycle and "the deliberate building of new structures and faculties" with the key words for Cancer, Leo and Virgo being *deciding*, *expressing* and *improving*. When the Sun enters Libra at the autumn equinox, the opposition, or maximum point of objective realisation has been reached, and the waning period begins. The key words for Libra, Scorpio and Sagittarius are *realising*, *sharing* and *demonstrating*. When the Sun enters Capricorn at the winter solstice, the waning square signifies another point of crisis and re-polarisation, with the key words for Capricorn, Aquarius and Pisces being *revaluing*, *reorganising* and, finally, *releasing*.

So you can see that aspects will be interpreted differently, depending whether the aspect is waxing or waning. The waning trine, for example, has a Sagittarius theme, and is more mature in its expression than the waxing trine, with its more subjective Leo approach. It has more experience to pass on and to teach. The waning square has a Capricorn theme, and its function is to establish collective or social structures which will stand the test of time, whereas the challenge of the waxing square, with its Cancer theme, is to put down roots to support continued personal development. And I am sure you can easily appreciate the difference between a waxing semi-sextile, when the cycle reaches Taurus, and a waning semi-sextile, when the cycle reaches Pisces.

The lunar cycle follows exactly the same process, in eight distinct stages. Once again, the new Moon is symbolically related to 0° Aries, the waxing crescent occurring symbolically at 15° Taurus and the first quarter Moon occurring at 0° Cancer. The process continues with the Moon gradually growing in fullness through to the waxing gibbous phase at 15° Leo and final culmination at the full Moon, which is symbolically related to 0° Libra. After the full Moon, the waning phase begins and the waning gibbous phase of the Moon occurs at 15° Scorpio, the last quarter at 0° Capricorn, and the waning crescent at 15° Aquarius.

Dane Rudhyar has provided us with eight different personality types which reflect the eight different Moon phases – which are extremely interesting and helpful (see next page). Each of these phases describes a particular energetic orientation as the cycle develops, and it is worth taking this into account in every chart interpretation we do.

The Nature of Cycles

The Eight Phases of the Lunar Cycle

	Moon Phase Type	Key Word	WAXING PHASE	Symbolic Zodiac Position	Interpretation
1.	NEW	EMERGENCE	☌ to ∠	0°♈ to 15°♉	Instinctive, youthful, subjective, energetic, impulsive
2.	CRESCENT	EXPANSION	∠ to □	15°♉ to 0°♋	The impulse towards action, to overcome obstacles
3.	FIRST QUARTER	ACTION	□ to ⚼	0°♋ to 15°♌	A turning point or crisis – decisions and commitments to be made. Hard work and tenacity required.
4.	GIBBOUS	OVERCOMING	⚼ to ☍	15°♌ to 0°♎	Perseverance. Adjustment to everyday realities.
			WANING PHASE		
5.	FULL	FULFILMENT	☍ to ⚼	0°♎ to 15°♏	Culmination. Objectivity and detachment.
6.	DISSEMINATING	DEMONSTRATION	⚼ to □	15°♏ to 0°♑	Maturity and generosity. Sharing experiences with others.
7.	LAST QUARTER	RE-ORIENTATION	□ to ∠	0°♑ to 15°♒	The challenge to eliminate what has served its purpose and become obsolete.
8.	BALSAMIC	RELEASE	∠ to ☌	15°♒ to 0°♓	A period of rest, reflection and letting go, so that the next cycle can begin afresh.

So, the first thing to do is to work out from your own chart whether you are a waxing Moon type or a waning Moon type – this could be very revealing.

Audience: I have the Sun is at 12° Virgo and the Moon at 25° Virgo, so that would mean I was born just after a new Moon?

Clare: Yes, you are a new Moon type – and because the Moon is less than 30° ahead of the Sun, it is symbolically in Aries – which means that you are likely to be excited about the world, and your fundamental approach will be impulsive, enthusiastic, instinctive, subjective, spontaneous and perhaps rather naive? Do you feel that?

Audience: Yes, that is interesting because I don't have any planets in Aries or in the first house but I can certainly feel that, so this makes sense to me.

Audience: I have Sun at 10° Scorpio and Moon at 22° Aquarius, so how do I work out my lunar phase?

Clare: The best way is first to work out whether your Moon is waxing or waning – and then to calculate the number of degrees between the Sun and Moon. In your case, the Moon is 102° ahead of the Sun, so it is waxing. It is more than 90° but less than 120° so it is in the first quarter phase, having symbolically reached 12° Cancer – the 'deciding' phase of the cycle – a time to establish and consolidate, to put down your roots and begin to actualise your potential in the world. At this stage in the cycle, we need to create a structure to support our continued development, which occurs during the gibbous phase, the waxing sesqui-quadrate, which begins symbolically at 15° Leo.

Audience: Do you know the meaning of the word 'gibbous', Clare?

Clare: Yes, it means pregnant. So it is a pregnant Moon, visually a bulging Moon, growing in size. So the waxing gibbous phase is a time to persevere and to pay attention to practical matters. At the full Moon, or opposition, symbolically equivalent to 0° Libra, the cycle has reached its maximum clarity and objectivity – its result. The plant has grown from seed through all the different phases and is now flowering.

During the waning phase the planets go through the same stages in reverse, but this is a more mature phase, distributing what has been learned, making final adjustments and laying the foundation for the future. People born during the waning phase tend to give of themselves and pass on their personal experience for the benefit of others and of society.

The disseminating phase begins symbolically at 15° Scorpio and includes the whole sign of Sagittarius, so it is the phase where knowledge and wisdom and experience are disseminated, or shared with others. The last quarter Moon phase, symbolically from 0° Capricorn to 15° Aquarius, begins with the waxing square, another turning point, a crisis in consciousness, a redefinition and the need to establish structures which will stand the test of time. The final balsamic phase, from the waning semi-square to the conjunction, symbolically includes the entire sign of Pisces. This phase is about letting go of the current cycle and preparing for the future cycle to come, so it involves surrender and sacrifice, but is also a period of gestation for the future cycle to come.

Audience: My Sun is at 5° Scorpio and my Moon is at 15° Cancer, so the Moon is waning and 110° behind the Sun. So what lunar phase am I?

Clare: Your Moon is more than 90° behind the Sun, so it has not yet reached the last quarter Moon phase. It is a disseminating Moon, symbolically at 10° Sagittarius. So I would imagine that your fundamental orientation is to explore, to travel and to teach?

Audience: That's right, I am a teacher, and have always enjoyed teaching, although I don't have anything in the ninth house or in Sagittarius.

Clare: So I hope these examples have demonstrated the significance of the lunar phase type, but more than that, looking at angular relationships in this way helps us to start seeing the natal chart in terms of a dynamic picture of unfolding cycles, rather than just a static map.

Audience: Did you say that this pattern is the same for all planetary pairs?

Clare: That's right. Let's use the Mercury-Jupiter cycle to illustrate this. Mercury moves around the zodiac with the Sun, so its cycle is about a year. Jupiter's orbit is around 12 years, so it spends approximately one year in each sign. This means that the Mercury-Jupiter cycle is around 13 months, and every one of us is born at a particular point in the Mercury-Jupiter cycle, whether or not there is an actual aspect between them.

The seed point of that cycle, or conjunction, will have occurred before birth and each one of us will be carrying a particular expression of that cycle, the meaning of which is the fundamental 'idea' which was planted at the conjunction. In fact you can trace back in the ephemeris to see exactly when and where that conjunction took place in your own chart, and even though that occurred before you were born, you are carrying that idea, which will be an expression of the meaning of the two planets themselves according to the sign and house in which it occurred. So how would we interpret the combined meaning of Mercury and Jupiter?

Audience: Big ideas or grand ideas.

Audience: Philosophical thinking.

Audience: Expansive or religious thought.

Audience: Exaggeration.

Audience: Lots of learning.

Audience: Exploring ideas.

Clare: Yes. So every one of us is carrying one particular expression of a grand or meaningful idea which was 'planted' before we were born at the pre-natal Mercury-Jupiter conjunction. As the faster planet, Mercury, begins to move away ahead of Jupiter, it will be absorbing information, studying and learning during the waxing phase. At the waxing square phase that idea needs to take root and become established in some way – it is time to consolidate. So the question is, what are we going to do with it, given that it is still growing? Perhaps this is time to go to school, or university, or to get a qualification which will take the idea further. That is the challenge of the waxing square. If we are born with a Mercury opposition to Jupiter then this is the culmination of the seed idea contained in the pre-natal conjunction, the maximum personal development and realisation of the seed idea, and another turning point in the cycle. If we are born with Mercury in the waning phase, there is likely to be more focus on distributing and sharing the ideas contained in the seed moment, such as teaching, or as the cycle begins to run out of steam we might prefer to work voluntarily or for a charity, since in this phase of the cycle we are no longer interested in learning anything new or in gaining anything for ourselves personally. Do you see how this might work?

Audience: I am confused, are you talking about the natal or transiting Mercury-Jupiter pair?

Clare: I am suggesting that you find out where the pre-natal conjunction of Mercury and Jupiter occurred in your chart so that you can understand where your big ideas and beliefs come from, and which phase of the Mercury-Jupiter cycle was active when you were born. But I am also talking, in essence, about the general astrological interpretation of cycles.

Audience: So it is like getting on a bus after it has already begun its journey. Right from the start it had a particular intention and a purpose and a goal and a direction, and you join that somewhere along the route.

Clare: Exactly.

Audience: So the seed moment of every planetary pair will have occurred before we were born?

Clare: Yes, because we are born at a particular stage of each planetary pair cycle. Using the Sun and Moon as examples, the degree, sign and natal house where that occurred will carry meaning, even though it is not marked on our charts. In fact it would be worth marking that point into your chart. That was the position of the alchemical *coniunctio*, the mystical marriage between the male and female principles, the symbolic conception point of our natal Moon phase.

Audience: I find this really interesting.

RETROGRADE MOTION

We will start looking at the specific cycles next week, but before we end today I would like to introduce you to the phenomenon of the apparent retrograde motion of all the planets except for the Sun and Moon. This is an optical illusion caused by the fact that our viewpoint is geocentric. We measure the position of planets against the backdrop of the stars and it is against this backdrop that planets appear to slow down, become stationary (known as stationary retrograde) and start moving backwards before slowing down again, becoming stationary (known as stationary direct) and moving forwards once more. That is the evidence of our eyes, even though we know that retrograde motion is, in fact, an illusion.

The other major optical illusion caused by our geocentric viewpoint is the Sun's daily movement. We experience the Sun rising in the east, climbing higher in the sky, culminating in the south at noon and then gradually dropping until it sets in the west, but of course it is not the Sun which is moving but the earth spinning on its axis which creates this illusion.

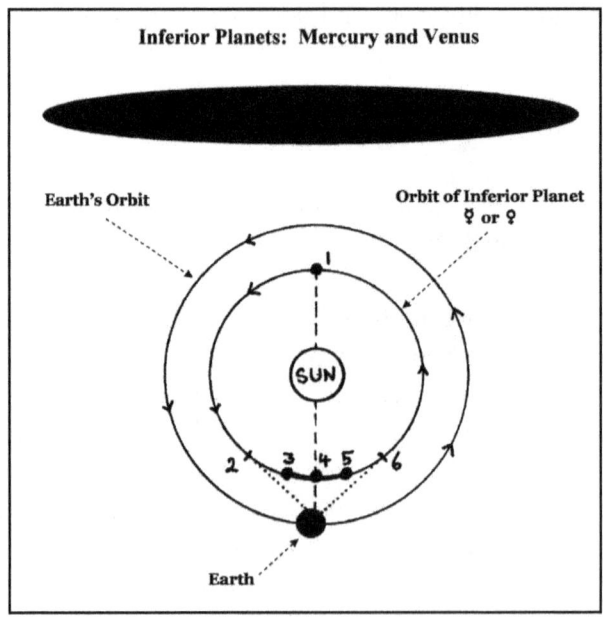

Audience: Can you illustrate how retrograde motion works?

Clare: Yes, I have some diagrams to show you, because it is hard to grasp without seeing it visually. There are two slightly different diagrams, one for the inferior planets, Mercury and Venus, which have orbits inside the Earth, and one for the superior planets which lie outside the orbit of the Earth. Let's start with the retrograde motion of the inferior planets.

Retrograde Motion of the Inferior Planets
When we are observing the orbits of Mercury and Venus we are facing towards the Sun, since Mercury can never be more than 27° from the Sun and Venus can never be more than 48° from the Sun. These angles are referred to as *angles of maximum elongation*, either east (2) or west (6) of the Sun. Mercury and Venus are retrograde 20% and 7% respectively mean average time.

The direct motion of all the planets from a geocentric view is anti-clockwise, viewed against the backdrop of the stars. You can see from the diagram that there are two kinds of conjunctions of Mercury and Venus with the Sun. When these planets are directly behind the Sun they are in superior conjunction (1), and their motion is direct. When Mercury and Venus are directly in front of the Sun they are in inferior conjunction (4), at their closest point to the Earth, and their motion is always retrograde. So they are invisible when they are conjunct, either hidden behind or in front of the Sun.

So, following the orbit of Mercury and Venus from superior conjunction (1) they continue direct until they reach their angles of maximum elongation east of the Sun (2). At this point, both planets are evening stars, setting after the Sun. Shortly afterwards, both Mercury and Venus appear to slow down and become stationary (3) and are always retrograde (3-5) at an inferior conjunction (4) with the Sun. They will then appear to slow down again and become stationary (5) before appearing to move direct once again, and reaching their greatest western elongation (6), when both planets are morning stars, rising before the Sun.

Audience: I can understand the mechanism, but it is really hard to visualise.

Clare: One way to think about this is to imagine you are driving around a roundabout in the middle of a forest. You are on the outside lane and there is another car travelling on the inside lane. Both cars are travelling forwards, but as you catch up and overtake the car on the inside lane, it will seem to stop and start travelling backwards for a while – when measured against the background trees. And there will also come a point when that car on the inside will appear to start moving forwards again. A similar thing happens with Chiron and the superior planets Mars, Jupiter, Saturn, Uranus, Neptune and Pluto.

Retrograde Motion of the Superior Planets

The mean average periods of retrogradation of the outer planets is 9% for Mars, 30% for Jupiter, 36% for Saturn, 41% for Uranus, 33% for Neptune and 44% for Pluto.

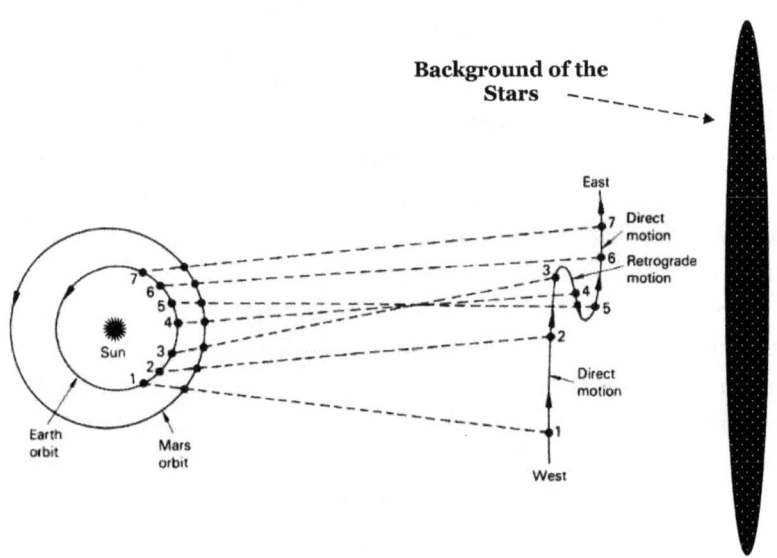

Viewed again from the Earth, the superior planet first appears to be in direct motion (1), then stationary (2) before going retrograde (3) and once again stationary (4) before continuing on its direct motion (5). The apparent retrograde motion of the superior planets occurs when the Sun and the superior planet are on opposite sides of the chart. It is therefore impossible for a superior planet to be in opposition to the Sun and not be retrograde.

Using our roundabout analogy again, we can say that this time you are driving on the inside lane and there is another car going around with you on the outside lane. Because you are inside, you are catching up, and as you do this the car on the outside lane will appear to stop and start moving backwards – when measured against the trees in the background – even though we know that it is still going forwards.

Audience: Is there a different interpretation when a planet is retrograde?

Clare: Yes, and the interpretation is really what you would imagine it to be. Planets which are direct tend to have a more direct expression outwards, motivated to engage with the world and with other people. Retrograde planets tend to be more reflective, contemplative and subjective, finding their motivation from deep within the individual. When a planet is changing direction and stationary, its energy is concentrated heavily in one single degree of the birth chart, which will be a point of great intensity and emphasis. I would certainly suggest that you have a look at your own charts to see how fast each planet is moving in its orbit at the time of your birth. This will provide useful information about the levels of power and intensity of the planets in your chart. Planets about to turn retrograde can have an obsessive quality about them, a concentrated intensity. Planets about to turn direct tend to have a quality of urgency and anticipation.

Notes
1. Charles Harvey, *Mundane Astrology*, p.137.
2. Leyla Rael & Dane Rudhyar, *Astrological Aspects: A Process Oriented Approach*. Preface, pp.i-ii.

LESSON 3

Introduction to Transits

For the next few weeks we are going to explore three 'real time' forecasting techniques – transits, solar returns and eclipses – and then we will move on to two symbolic time techniques – secondary progressions and solar arc directions. And these will certainly be enough for us to be getting on with at the moment.

It is important to remember that all these techniques are based on the birth chart, and none of them make any sense unless they are related back to the birth chart, which should always be our anchor. Otherwise it is all too easy to get carried away with a technique and become disorientated and lose perspective. Once we have the birth chart, we can calculate the exact date of every transit, progression, direction, solar return and eclipse which is ever going to occur in the life of the individual.

Audience: So it is like a symphony which has already been written, but has yet to be played out by the orchestra?

Clare: Exactly, although the interpretation of the piece is up to us, and we don't yet know whether the instruments are out of tune, whether the musicians can read music, or whether the conductor is capable of bringing the whole piece together into a harmonious whole. This is another way of saying that the task, or entelechy, of an acorn is to become an oak tree, and no matter how hard the acorn wishes to grow into a sycamore tree, it will fail. As Jung said: "Free will is the ability to do gladly that which I must do."

Real Time Forecasting: Transits
The birth chart is the structural map of our lives, fixed at a moment in time/space, but of course the planets continue on their journeys after birth, transiting around the chart. Transits are the most well known of all the astrological forecasting techniques. They can be defined as the actual movement of the planets in 'actual', 'real' time, and the planetary positions on any day are identical for everyone on Earth.

It is very important – and very difficult – to realise that transits are not *being done to us*, although that is what it feels like. Transits need to be used actively and creatively. They are times when the planetary deities speak to us, reminding us that there is work to be done, and indicating the nature of that work. It is useful to ask ourselves, 'What is the meaning of this?' and 'What am I being asked to learn and how can I use this?', since all transits carry the potential for change, growth and increased self knowledge and self awareness. It is important not to waste these opportunities but to actively engage with our transits, solar returns and eclipses. No matter how fated they may feel, it is unhelpful to take a passive position and fall into the trap of thinking there is nothing we can do about them. After all, we are the only species, as far as we know, which has an opportunity to actively and consciously grasp the kairos.

Each transiting planet carries a specific quality of dynamic energy, defined by the natal position of that planet, but active only for a certain period of time. So for example, if we have a Mars transit then it is telling us to act. With a Saturn transit we may need to learn to wait. A Neptune transit suggests that we let things drift for a while. They are gifts, messages, clues and hints.

Audience: You said that the transit carries the energy of its natal position?

Clare: Yes, and this is why we all respond differently to the same transit, since all transiting planets carry their natal imprint and natal tuning with them. So a Mars transit is not just a Mars transit – it is an opportunity for us to learn more about our own personal capacity and ability to assert ourselves and achieve our goals, which will be described by the sign, house and aspects of our natal Mars. This is an important point.

Audience: Can you give us an example of this, Clare?

Clare: Let's say that three people are having a Mars transit to their Sun. The first person has natal Mars in Aries trine Jupiter in Sagittarius, so the Mars transit will carry tremendous positive – perhaps excessive – energy, an urge to travel, to expand their horizons, to search for meaning, and an impulse of increased faith and optimism. The second person has natal Mars in Capricorn square Saturn, so the Mars transit will bring with it the opportunity for focus and hard work to achieve their goals. The nature of that work and the nature of those goals would be indicated by the house and planet which Mars is currently transiting. The third person might have natal Mars conjunct Uranus in Libra. Transiting Mars is likely to bring with it unexpected and sudden meetings or separations, according to the house and planet which Mars is currently transiting.

In order to work with transits we need to remember the orbit times of the planets, and therefore their relative speeds, and how to find out where they are at any particular time. And this is where the ephemeris is particularly useful, since it provides us with the whole story – all the information we need to find out the past, current or future zodiacal position of any planet, when and for how long it is retrograde, the Moon's phases and the eclipses. The ephemeris is the astrologers' bible and I really encourage you to carry one with you at all times.

	AVERAGE ORBIT TIME	TRANSIT: Average daily motion of the Planets
SUN		1° degree per day
MOON	28 days (orbits the earth)	11°47' – 15°12' per day
MERCURY	88 days	Maximum speed 2° per day Goes ℞ 3 times a year, slowing down considerably before changing direction.
VENUS	225 days	Maximum speed 1°12' per day Goes ℞ no more than once a year, and some years not at all. Slows down considerably before changing direction
MARS	687 days	30' – 40' a day Goes ℞ approximately every two years Slows down considerably before changing direction
JUPITER	11.86 years	Maximum 14' per day Goes ℞ once a year for as long as 4 months
SATURN	29.46 years	Maximum 7' per day Goes ℞ once a year for as long as 5 months
URANUS	84 years	2 – 5' per day Goes ℞ once a year for more than 5 months
NEPTUNE	165 years	Maximum 2' per day Goes ℞ once a year for more than 5 months
PLUTO	248 years	Maximum 2' per day Goes ℞ once a year for more than 5 months

So we have some very different planetary speeds here. The Moon transits the entire chart every month, which means that it spends about 2½ days transiting each sign, which equates to about 1° every two hours. And of course the Moon rules our moods and we all know how changeable they are. As the Moon shifts from one house to another, or from one sign to another our moods change, and it is a good exercise to record your own moods throughout an entire month, and watch how they change.

So we cannot give anything like the same weight to the transiting Moon as we would to transiting Neptune or Pluto, which move a maximum 2' per day and are retrograde for more than five months of each year. The transiting Moon reinforces our habits and emotional patterns but does not indicate any kind of significant change in our lives. A transit of Mars will act as a trigger and might indicate some kind of action, or an argument, but it will not change our lives. The transits of the planets from Saturn out to Pluto, on the other hand, can bring profound life changes. So we need to take account of the relative speed of each planet in order to get our emphasis right. And for this reason our main focus as far as transits are concerned will be on the planets from Mars outwards.

I like to think of the transits as music, as an expression of the harmony of the spheres, with the higher notes being played by the faster moving planets, and successively lower notes being played by the successively slower moving planets, which set the background theme or rhythm for the melody which is played on top.

Since all the planets, except the Sun and Moon, have periods of retrograde motion, transits, particularly of the outer three planets, can form three, and sometimes five conjunctions – direct, retrograde, direct – and will therefore last for a considerable time. The further away the planet is from the Sun, the longer the transit is likely to last.

Triple conjunctions are like recurring dreams – it is as if the psyche is trying particularly hard to get a message through to us, since we will have the conjunction not once, not twice but three times. So we need to pay even more attention than normal to the planetary message. The first direct conjunction is normally experienced in projection, as coming at us from the outside world or from another person, as nothing to do with us. At the retrograde conjunction we can internalise and begin to process the meaning of the transit, perhaps to take more responsibility and to make adjustments. And by the time of the final direct conjunction we will hopefully have learned more about the natal potential of that planet, and may well have changed our attitude, which will stand us in good stead for the future.

Audience: Can you give us an example of a triple conjunction transit?

Clare: Assume, for example, that we have a natal Saturn square Moon, and that Saturn is making three transits to our Sun. So we need to ask first of all, 'What is the purpose of this transit?' The Sun, symbol of our core identity, is being acted on by Saturn, and so – to the extent that we are willing to accept the wisdom and knowledge which the god is offering – its purpose is to help us become more realistic, more mature and to emerge with a sense of enhanced personal authority. To understand the specific themes, we need to focus on the natal Moon-Saturn square, since Saturn will bring that Moon square with it.

We know that the Saturn-Moon pair rule the opposite signs of Capricorn and Cancer and relate to the parent/child relationship so this transit will trigger memories of our early childhood and of our parents, and these memories are likely to be painful and challenging since this is, after all, a square.

The first transiting conjunction of Saturn to the Sun is likely to be experienced as an outside event, as some kind of rejection and limitation and we may feel very alone and a deep sense of primal abandonment. At the following retrograde conjunction of Saturn to the Sun we have an opportunity to internalise and process this experience and realise that, with Saturn square Moon, we are perfectly capable of learning to take care of ourselves and of meeting our own needs, now that we are adult. By the time of the final direct conjunction, we may have 'grown up', become more emotionally mature and self sufficient.

Every transit has a purpose and carries a personal message if we are prepared to ask the right questions and engage with what is going on. Our task as psychological astrologers is to actively engage with each transit, to ask the right questions and to internalise the experience. We can always decide not to do this, of course, in which case the transits will be lived out unconsciously in the form of projection onto others or onto the outside world, and the opportunity for increased self knowledge will be missed.

It can take a while to recognise what is actually happening with these transits because, although they present opportunities for our conscious growth and expansion, they are often experienced in the first instance as the exact opposite, and this is worth remembering as we work with clients.

For example, a Jupiter transit tells us that it is time to venture beyond our existing confines, to expand our horizons and seek something more meaningful. But we would not have the impetus, courage or energy to embark on this journey unless we were feeling increasingly trapped and restless and so restricted by outer circumstances that we were beginning to feel overwhelmed by panic or even feel rather manic – both manifestations of a trapped Jupiter. But if we can sit with the meaning of Jupiter for a while, then we will realise that we would not be feeling this way at all unless it was time to expand and find wider, more meaningful, horizons.

Transits of the Outer Planets
It is only something over 230 years since Uranus was discovered in 1781, 160 years in the case of Neptune, which was discovered in 1846, and less than 100 years in the case of Pluto, which was discovered in 1930. So it is only in relatively recent times that astrologers have had to include the outer planets and their transits in their work.

Until their discovery, we could say that the influence of the outer planets was simply projected onto supernatural forces – both divine and demonic. For example, the sudden revelations, visions and unexpected changes we now associate with Uranus were more likely to be understood as epiphanies, or 'acts of God'. The human capacity for unconditional love and compassion which we now associate with Neptune was more likely to be seen as emanating from a divine source than from a human source. Equally, the dark forces of evil, destruction, bestiality and lust, were projected onto external devils 'out there'.

Now that our solar system has expanded to include these outer planets, that means they are also in our birth charts, which means of course that they are aspects of our own human psyches. This makes our task more complicated, since we now have to find a personal relationship with the outer planets as an aspect of the evolution of consciousness itself. As Jung said: "The psychological rule says that when an inner situation is not made conscious, it happens outside as fate."[1]

> "Therefore the individual who wishes to have an answer to the problem of evil, has need, first and foremost of *self-knowledge*, that is, the utmost possible knowledge of his own wholeness. He must know relentlessly how much good he can do, and what crimes he is capable of, and must beware of regarding the one as real and the other as illusion. Both are elements within his nature, and both are bound to come to light in him, should he wish – as he ought – to live without self deception or self-delusion."[2]

Audience: This reminds me of a book I once read called the *A Wizard of Earthsea*.[3] It was basically about a boy who discovers he has magical powers. I don't remember the details now, but he releases this dark thing from under the earth, and spends many years running away from it. But it follows him everywhere and exhausts him and takes every part of his energy out of him, until the time comes when he is united with it, then he regains his strength. It was interesting, because the only thing he had released was his own darker side. It is a really brilliant story.

Clare: Yes, and that story is a good example of the importance of our approach to the transits of the outer planets. It would be a mistake to think we can 'use' these transits as we would use the transits of the planets out to Saturn. Although they are personal, to the extent that they are in each of our birth charts, they also carry transpersonal, generational themes and their purpose and function is collective and therefore beyond the control of our individual wills and egos. Our ego control structures are carefully constructed to keep us safe and to resist change, to stay with what we know, no matter how ultimately unfulfilling and unsatisfactory that might be. This is why the way we engage with these outer planet transits is particularly important.

The function of Uranus, Neptune and Pluto seems to be to eliminate, shatter and dissolve the defence structures we have created but – and this is crucial – only those structures which have become stuck, or rigid or outgrown and are no longer relevant or serving life itself. So there are several key questions we need to ask ourselves when we are experiencing transits of the outer planets.

Uranus transits bring new levels of awareness, insight and perspective which enable us to break old patterns and free ourselves from habitual assumptions which have become limiting or inappropriate. The question we might ask under a Uranus transit is, 'What old patterns or assumptions are no longer appropriate?' and 'Where do I need to break free of old, outworn patterns?' To the extent that we refuse the gift of the Uranus transit and resist change, we will lose the opportunity for increased objectivity and our thinking is likely to become more rigid, fearful and defended.

Under Neptune transits our old gods die and we can find ourselves in the wilderness where we feel lost and abandoned and everything seems meaningless. This can be an intensely painful experience, a period of uncertainty, confusion and disillusion as our false dreams, fantasies and illusions are dissolved. But it also means that they are ready to be replaced by more appropriate ideals and dreams and eventually, after a period of mourning, there will be new gods and dreams which will be capable of sustaining us in the future. Questions we might ask under a Neptune transit are, 'What does my soul long for now?' and 'How can I realise and fulfil my emerging dreams?'

With transits of Pluto we find ourselves unexpectedly confronted with power struggles, feelings of being manipulated and controlled and, before we know it, deep and primitive survival instincts are constellated as we find ourselves dragged into a black hole of obsession. Pluto demands regeneration by eliminating and purging that which has been outgrown or become poisonous to the system. The useful questions to ask in the face of a Pluto transit are, 'How and where have I been giving away my true power or life force?', 'What has been outgrown and now no longer serves the deeper purpose of my life?', 'What needs to be purged, exorcised or eliminated?' and 'Where and how do I find the courage to let go and trust and enter the unknown?'

Audience: In one sense I can cope with this perfectly well, but what do you actually mean by ego boundaries? Where is your ego?

Clare: The ego can be described as our socially adjusted persona, the mask we have developed in order to be acceptable to ourselves and to others. It is the label we wear when we present ourselves to the world.

The point is that, in the process of becoming socially adjusted, we actually have to differentiate between what is acceptable and what is not acceptable, and we normally use social conventions and values as our benchmark. So that personal traits which are unacceptable to our view of ourselves do not get incorporated into our ego structure, but are projected instead. So if I am identified with being a good girl, then bad behaviour belongs to other people and not to me. This is fairly basic stuff.

Audience: So you go looking for the bad in others in order to make you feel good? Is that one way of dealing with it, 'I don't do that so I am alright'?

Clare: Yes, that's right.

Audience: Isn't there a more positive side to the ego, in the sense that you need a shape, so that other people know who you are, even though they might only see your conscious persona?

Clare: Absolutely. But the point is, do we actually identify with our socially adapted roles or not? Does our sense of ourselves depend upon them? Are they something we wear casually and comfortably, with a good sense of humour and self-deprecation, or are they roles that we identify with and cling to? If our ego boundaries are strong but flexible, then we can navigate the transits of the outer planets more consciously and creatively. But if our ego is a rigid and tightly defended structure, then there are three ways we are likely to react to the transits of the outer planets, none of which will help us in the end. Firstly, the ego may well try and identify with the transiting planet, in which case we will become inflated – omnipotent in the case of Pluto, omnipresent in the case of Neptune and omniscient in the case of Uranus.

Secondly, we might deny the transit altogether and carry on as if nothing had happened, in which case it will be projected onto the world or onto other people and we will have missed the opportunity for increased personal consciousness.

Thirdly, we may sense the impending disruption to our existing structures and do everything in our power to defend ourselves against the changes which carry the possibility of increased self knowledge and wholeness. We may seek to regress to a time when everything felt safer. It is all too easy to recognise when people have decided to stop growing and become rigid, brittle and defensive, both physically, emotionally and mentally. Such people know where they stand and choose to remain carefully within the boundaries of what they already know. The skin will not stretch any more and there will be no more growth, which means that other people and the outside world will become increasingly negative and threatening. Needless to say, we are unlikely to meet them in our consulting rooms.

Audience: Say that you have a personal planet in aspect to an outer planet. Does that mean you are particularly open to the collective?

Clare: I think it means that you will have to work with that particular collective energy the whole time. A weak ego structure is inflated, grandiose and narcissistic, and particularly prone to being overwhelmed by these collective forces.

Audience: So if you expand the boundaries of your ego to include the outer planet, without identifying with it, then the meaning of the whole thing changes?

Clare: Yes, and that is the challenge of Saturn. If we can consciously embrace and include more collective awareness within our ego boundary, without identifying with it, then that might be a good definition of wisdom – the recognition that we are part of the whole and the acceptance that this does not have to be within our control.

Audience: It is strange in a way, that it might take you half a lifetime to find out who you are and what you are really like, but then you are still open to other possibilities for expansion. It seems like a paradox.

Clare: That's right and once we have a paradox then we know we are getting closer to the truth. A highly evolved and mature ego is soft and gentle and lightly held, able to accept, and even enjoy, paradox without feeling threatened.

We already know that the outer planets carry generational themes, according to the sign they were in at our birth. Here is a table showing the transits of the outer planets through the signs from the beginning of the 20th century. The asterisks refer to the retrograde motion of the planets back into the previous sign.

Outer Planets in Signs[5]

	URANUS	NEPTUNE	PLUTO
Average Time Spent in a Sign	7 Years	14 Years	20 Years
ARIES	Apr 1927 * Nov 1927 Jan 1928		
TAURUS	Sep 1934 * Oct 1934 Mar 1935		
GEMINI	May 1942		
CANCER	June 1949	Jul 1901 * Dec 1901 May 1902	Sep 1912 * Oct 1912 Jul 1913 * Dec 1913 May 1914
LEO	Aug 1955 * Jan 1956 June 1956	Sep 1914 * Dec 1914 July 1915 * Mar 1916 May 1916	Oct 1937 * Nov 1937 Aug 1938 * Feb 1939 June 1939
VIRGO	Aug 1962	Sep 1928 * Feb 1929 July 1929	Oct 1956 * Jan 1957 Aug 1957 * Apr 1958 June 1958
LIBRA	Sep 1968 * May 1969 June 1969	Oct 1942 * Apr 1943 Aug 1943	Oct 1971 * Apr 1972 Jul 1972
SCORPIO	Nov 1974 * May 1975 Sep 1975	Oct 1956 * June 1957 Aug 1957	Nov 1983 * May 1984 Aug 1984
SAGITTARIUS	Nov 1981	Nov 1970	Jan 1995 * Apr 1995 Nov 1995
CAPRICORN	Feb 1988 * May 1988 Dec 1988	Jan 1984 * June 1984 Nov 1984	Jan 2008 * June 2008 Nov 2008

AQUARIUS	Apr 1995 * June 1995 Jan 1996	Jan 1998 * Aug 1998 Nov 1998	Mar 2023 * June 2023 Jan 2024 * July 2024 Nov 2024
PISCES	Mar 2003 * Sep 2003 Dec 2003	April 2011 * Aug 2011 Feb 2012	
ARIES	May 2010 * Aug 2010 Mar 2011	Mar 2025 * Oct 2025 Jan 2026	
TAURUS	May 2018 *Nov 2018 Mar 2019		

Notes
1. C.G. Jung, *Aion*, Collected Works Volume 9, p.126.
2. C.G. Jung, *Memories, Dreams and Reflections*, p.330.
3. Ursula K. Le Guin, *A Wizard of Earthsea*.
4. Neil F. Michelsen, *Tables of Planetary Phenomena*.

LESSON 4

Transits of the Outer Planets

PLUTO, NEPTUNE, URANUS AND CHIRON

Clare: When I am interpreting a chart I find it useful to start with the transits of the outer planets and work gradually down in scale, so this is what we are going to do this evening. The longer the orbit, the deeper the musical note, so the outer planets provide the all important backdrop against which to measure the transits of the faster planets. There are cycles within cycles occurring all the time, but the transits of the outer planets are so powerful that they can sometimes 'drown out' the transits of the faster moving planets.

In addition, the outer planet transits tell us immediately what age our client is and which astrological era they belong to, which helps us put our forecasting work into context. Charles Harvey wrote that "the deeper significance and purpose of our own lives can only really be understood when seen in the context of the major cycles of which our lives are a particular expression."[1]

> "Each one of us is, to a greater or lesser extent, the product of our own period of history. Just as our nationality, culture, sex, race, heredity and family background are important indicators as to how we will meet the world, so equally the larger generational planetary patterns give crucial clues as to the larger raison d'etre of our own unique place in the mosaic of consciousness."[2]

Pluto Transits

As with all transits, we need to begin by assessing the planet's natal meaning, by sign, house and aspects. This will help us understand the transit itself.

The meaning of our natal Pluto can lie dormant for many years – a dumb note in the chart. So Pluto's transits can often take us by surprise, since they are so intense and uncompromising. They tend to be experienced as an eruption of unconscious, archaic, primitive emotions. Naturally, this can be an extremely frightening experience for the ego, part of which is being forced to die, like a carapace which has outlived its purpose and must be discarded if the new life within is to be released. When the forces of change begin to emerge from deep within our unconscious, they are initially experienced in projection. Primitive forces are constellated 'out there' and there is a reinforcement of the ego structures against the 'enemy'. With transits of Pluto we find ourselves unexpectedly confronted with power struggles, feelings of being manipulated and controlled, and before we know it, deep and primitive survival instincts are constellated as we find ourselves dragged into a black hole of obsession.

Pluto demands regeneration by eliminating and purging that which has been outgrown or become poisonous to the system. We can all too easily fall into the passive trap of assuming that, for example, such and such is happening *because* of a Pluto transit, but a more useful and creative attitude and approach as I suggested last week, would be to ask: 'What is this great god of the underworld asking of me now? What is it that I have outgrown and need to let go of, since it no longer serves the deeper purpose of my life? Where am I no longer prepared to give away my true power and life force? Where do I have to be absolutely honest and purge, exorcise and eliminate old emotional rubbish which no longer serves me? Where and how do I need to find the courage to let go and trust and enter the unknown?'

Pluto spends an average of 20 years in a sign, which means that the waxing square to natal Pluto would normally occur around the age of 60 and the opposition at the age of 120. Pluto has an extremely elliptical orbit, taking around 30 years to transit through the sign of Taurus, when it is at its furthest point from the earth, and around eleven years to transit through the signs of Libra and Scorpio, when it is closest to the Earth and inside the orbit of Neptune. This has had a profound effect on recent generations – people born in the last half of the 20th century, which includes most of us. Have a look at this table:

Date of Birth	Natal Pluto	Pluto Waxing Square	Pluto Opposition
1940	Leo	45	85
1950	Leo	41	84
1960	Virgo	37	86
1970	Virgo	36	93
1980	Libra	38	106
1990	Scorpio	45	–

So you can see from this table that if you were born in 1940 then the Pluto square Pluto will have occurred at the age of 45 – which is 15 years earlier than the average. If you were born in 1950 the Pluto square will occur at the age of 41, and if you are born in 1960 or 1970 then the square will occur even earlier, at the ages of 37 or 36.

Audience: So if you were born in the '50s or '60s, then you might live to see your Pluto opposition?

Clare: Yes, that's right, provided you live into your 80s. And this phenomenon only occurs for a few decades in each Pluto cycle, or once every 248 years. You can also see from the table that people born with Pluto in Libra and Scorpio will have a relatively early Pluto square but, as Pluto begins to slow down as it moves through Sagittarius and Capricorn, they are unlikely to live until their Pluto opposition. And this is psychologically significant, not least because transiting Pluto square natal Pluto now occurs during the same years as the midlife transits of the Neptune square Neptune and Uranus opposition Uranus.

Audience: What is the effect on the generations who are having to confront their Pluto square Pluto earlier? Do you think this explains the rise of psychotherapy and depth psychology?

Clare: That could well be the case. I suspect this means that we can no longer avoid confronting and purging the vast collective residue of unprocessed emotions in the way that previous generations have, and perhaps have had to have. We have been living in a very psychological age for the past fifty years, and many groups have been formed during this time to encourage people to explore and express their emotions and feelings. Pluto is about psychological depth and healing, and for those who lived before this era, particularly perhaps our parents, grandparents and great grandparents who lived through the two world wars, their experiences were too recent, too raw and painful to be able to process and heal. You can see from the table that Pluto entered Cancer at the beginning of the First World War, a time when old securities were destroyed and families throughout Europe were decimated, if not by the war itself then by the flu epidemic at the end of the war, which killed something like 20 million people. So the task of processing and healing these ancestral wounds has been inherited by subsequent generations.

Audience: That sounds like my mother. There is no way she will go anywhere near any kind of emotional processing. Not even near. And that means that I have had to do it, since the family stuff is just so heavy.

Clare: I suspect that many of us have inherited a sizeable amount of emotional healing work left over from previous generations. Perhaps this is the result of Pluto speeding up and bringing its square so early – it is as if Pandora's box has opened and we can no longer try and push everything back into the box.

Audience: In terms of emphasis, would transiting Pluto opposing, say, Saturn, have a stronger impact than a natal opposition of Saturn-Pluto? What kind of emphasis should we give to transits?

Clare: There will be a kind of familiarity with a natal aspect such as Pluto opposite Saturn. We get used to our own chart, we come to expect the repetition of certain themes and respond in a certain way to repeating patterns. Transits are different, because they constellate certain natal themes which may have been dormant, bring them to light and consciousness and therefore facilitate change and new awareness.

Audience: I am not exactly happy about this, since I will have Pluto transiting my seventh house in Capricorn for about 30 years. Hopefully I will meet a Pluto man who will stick around?

Audience: For 30 years. [laughter]

Clare: Pluto's transit of the seventh house will bring the natal meaning of Pluto to life. The transit will herald a new chapter of self discovery, constellated through your relationships. Pluto will expose any control issues or power games you or your partner might be playing. The seventh house will be your burning ground for the duration of this transit.

Audience: And I have the square now as well. I am 37.

Clare: Well, that is an excellent time for you to learn more about your natal Pluto. Pluto in our charts is where we bury everything which is primitive or socially taboo. But if we scratch the surface of Pluto, which is what occurs during a transit, then a whole host of primitive and savage emotions such as jealousy, obsession, paranoia and rage will erupt into our lives, carrying an intensity which has us in its grip and which we are often surprisingly reluctant to let go of.

Audience: I was surprised at the speed of the transit. It started last year, goes retrograde for a bit and is over by the end of this year. If people have a Pluto transit which lasts for several years, does that mean they will be in crisis all that time, or does it fizzle out?

Clare: Well, as I was saying last week, when an outer planet transit lasts several years it normally receives three hits – the planet transits three times, direct, retrograde and finally direct again. This allows for a gradual realisation and understanding of the emerging themes, since each transit brings more experience and knowledge. Usually the first transit brings the first awareness, the retrograde transit brings an opportunity to internalise and real-ise the meaning, and ideally the third transit brings a more mature understanding and conscious incorporation, so these long transits can in fact be extremely creative.

Audience (Janet): I am interested in this because I had my first Pluto square last year and it didn't mean anything particular to me. I think it hits again in August and again at the end of the year. I thought it would be dramatic, since it was Pluto, but I can't remember anything particular. I have been thinking that I have got off quite lightly, but I still have another two hits to go.

Clare: Then it is possible that your Pluto transit is initially being experienced in projection, which is often the case when people can't immediately relate to it themselves. Can we look at your Pluto? This will help us to understand what the themes are likely to be, since they will inevitably originate from the position of your natal Pluto.

Audience (Janet): Here it is – the Ascendant is 22° Virgo and Pluto is in Virgo in the twelfth house. It is opposite Chiron and trine to Mars in Aries in the eighth house. The Sun is in Cancer in the tenth house.

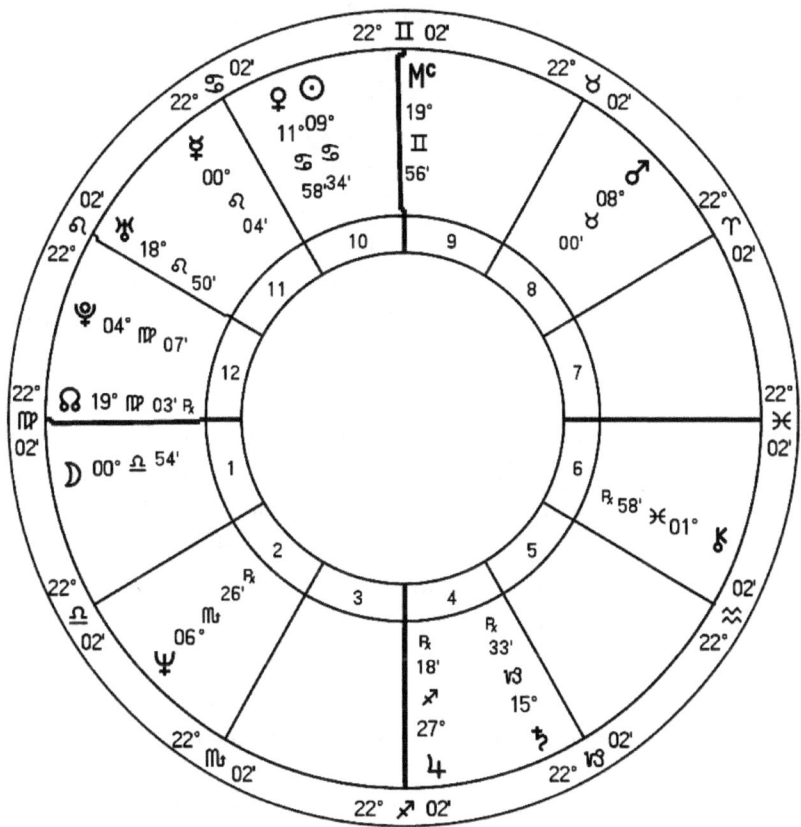

Janet: Data withheld for purposes of confidentiality

Clare: So transiting Pluto is going through your third house.

Audience (Janet): Yes.

Clare: Planets in the twelfth house describe inherited themes which are subtle and hard to get hold of but which can profoundly affect our lives. Since your Sun rules the twelfth house, we could say that your journey of self discovery will involve engaging with buried family themes of power and control, particularly since the Sun is in Cancer and in the parental house of the mother. The collective survival themes of the Pluto in Virgo generation concern health, work, food and the feminine generally, with particular emphasis on control, generated by an inherited feeling of the powerlessness of the feminine generally, and this is strongly exacerbated by the fact that Chiron is opposite Pluto in the sixth house. I suspect that the purpose of the Pluto square will be to loosen up some of this intense control, to connect you to the organic power of the feminine. In the end, you are a Cancerian, and your Libran Moon is far too civilised and rational to be much help at the moment.

With Pluto transiting the third house, you have an opportunity to find out more about this inheritance, and something might well be emerging, because the third house is about learning and understanding. Following the third house theme, it may be that this has to do with your siblings.

Janet: This is interesting, because I have been learning astrology since this transit started, so that certainly fits in. One of the things which has come out of my astrological studies is a greater interest in my family background, and I have become fascinated with families and family issues generally, so that would make perfect sense. I am trying to figure out what has been going on.

Clare: This is an excellent time for you to learn more about your family. Would you say there are lots of buried issues in the family?

Janet: I expect so, although I really have no idea. But the interesting thing is that my sister's family have recently all gone into family therapy, and none of us knows what is going on in there, nobody talks about it.

Even our mother, who always gossips about what is going on, has drawn a complete blank on this one.

Clare: The Pluto square Pluto transit can indicate that a metaphorical boil has formed on the skin, gathering the previously buried poison together under increasing pressure until it is ready to be lanced. There can be feelings of shame and even horror, since nobody wants to really look at the boil until they are forced to do so, but it seems as if this has now happened in your sister's family. Something needs to be recognised, purged and eliminated so that healthy growth can resume. It seems that your first Pluto square is being experienced in projection, in the form of your sister and her family but I suspect that, as the retrograde Pluto square and final direct Pluto square occur, something in the family history will come to light which will bring changes in your life too.

Audience (Janet): But is it possible to say: 'No thank you, Pluto' and not deal with it at all? Or does the boil just go on getting bigger?

Clare: Well, we know that with Pluto in the twelfth house, something has been building up over the generations, but there is no imperative which decrees that we have to engage with it. However, if you think of the mythology of Pluto, or Hades, god of the underworld, there is immense wealth and power there, as well as a great deal of sheer energy, raw vitality, the organic life force itself. It can be wonderful to be able to access that power as source of energy and personal potency.

I remember a client with natal Pluto in Leo in the seventh house, which indicates that relationships will tend to constellate themes to do with control and the balance of power. And because transiting Pluto was squaring her natal Pluto I asked her how her marriage was, and she said it was fine. So I then asked her if her husband had been going through any kinds of changes recently. I thought maybe that her Pluto square may be happening in projection but apparently her husband was perfectly happy and no particular changes were going on there.

So, what do we do when the client is telling us that nothing is happening and that everything is fine, but the astrology is telling us something else? Do we accept what the client tells us at face value, or do we pursue the astrological symbolism a bit further? One of the most useful things Charles Harvey taught me when I was a student, is to take a deep breath and trust what the astrology is telling us, although of course this has to be done with great sensitivity and respect. So I talked with my client about her natal seventh house Pluto, her need for passion and intensity in relationships and suggested that she might spend some more time with her husband or that they might go away together for a weekend, but clearly she felt that her marriage was fine and that there was no need. On the surface the marriage was happy but the Pluto square was telling a different story. Pluto transits are either black or white – there are no shades of grey. Either it is dormant or it is constellated in an intense and obsessive way. A few months later she returned. She told me she had discovered that her husband had been having an affair and wanted to leave the marriage. And then I worked for several years with her through Pluto's burning ground – she was consumed, obsessed, jealous, vengeful, enraged and, ultimately, very much alive.

With another client of mine the situation was reversed. Since becoming a mother, Barbara had been living busily and almost exclusively, it seemed, from her Virgo Moon conjunct MC. She was a full time mother, a breast-feeding counsellor and chair of the parent/teacher association. Her hobby was jewellery-making and she was practical, efficient and skilful, as only a Virgo Moon can be. Barbara's natal Pluto was in Leo, squaring a close Sun-Venus conjunction in Scorpio in the twelfth house, but this aspect was lying dormant under her adapted, efficient Virgo Moon persona. But the question is whether a happy marriage, three children, a respectable house in the suburbs and two cars on the drive is enough for a woman with a Sun-Venus conjunction in Scorpio in the twelfth house? When Pluto began to transit this Sun-Venus conjunction and square her natal Pluto, she suddenly became obsessed with one of the teachers at her children's school. All the sexual intensity and passion which had been missing from her life was constellated, and she decided she must have him at any cost. She started stalking him, in the grip of a full blown obsession. Have you seen the film *Fatal Attraction*? That's a very good example of how Pluto gets unleashed.

Audience: I have been there, and it is really frightening.

Clare: If you are working therapeutically with someone in a Pluto obsession, there is nothing to be done but to provide a safe hearth and wait for the fire to burn itself out. But the question is, what is the purpose of the Pluto transit? Although it can come like a bolt from the blue and be extremely disturbing, its purpose seems to be to awaken our own dormant power and vitality. Eventually, when the transit has passed, we will realise that we have been transformed by the experience, usually in very positive ways. Power is a pejorative word in our society, and yet in essence it describes the destructive and regenerative power in nature and in the universe, such as the energy of a volcanic eruption, or solar flares, or the birth and death of stars. Plutonic people, who have Scorpio rising, planets in Scorpio or in the eighth house, and an angular or heavily aspected Pluto in their charts, are agents of this process of constant collective destruction and regeneration. Of course we tend to be afraid of this, and try and control it, however unconsciously. Think about the house where Pluto is in your own charts, and consider if this is an area of life where you might be rather obsessive.

Audience: I have Pluto in my fifth house and I am definitely obsessed with my children. Perhaps I do try to dominate and control them too much. But trusting enough to let them go is very difficult for me.

Clare: That is a good example because, ultimately, you are going to have to let them go, whether you like it or not. The natural organic process is that they will grow up and leave home, and in fact you are also going to leave them, since you are likely to die before them. There is nothing personal about it.

Audience: Does that mean that if Pluto transits your Sun then you have to let go of the Sun?

Clare: A transit of Pluto to the Sun normally has the effect of burning off the dross, in terms of our false identity or false sense of self, which can be intensely painful at the time but which can lead to the emergence of a much more authentic sense of self.

Audience: I have a natal Sun-Pluto square, and I always feel as if I am constantly having to reinvent myself.

Clare: When Pluto is the ruler of the chart or aspecting any of our personal planets, life is meant to be a continual process of purging and regeneration – otherwise we become power demons and poison both ourselves and others.

Audience: I have Pluto transiting my Moon at the moment and my female boss is trying to control my life. She sabotages everything I do. But because she is my boss I am not sure how to deal with it.

Clare: This is a difficult problem, since the balance of power is not equal to begin with. Whenever we have a Pluto transit we tend to become hyper-sensitive to issues of power and control, and this is likely to be projected, but only to the extent that we have not owned our own power. Then we find ourselves in a survival struggle, feeling as if we are going to be annihilated or obliterated by circumstances or by other people. This is such a primitive, archaic, experience that it can feel like a psychic attack, and cannot really be dealt with rationally.

Audience: I am not sure I like what has been happening to me since this started. I have begun to feel spiteful and really nasty towards her, wishing that all sorts of calamities might befall her.

Clare: So this transit of Pluto on your Moon has revealed your dark emotions, and your capacity for rage and revenge, possibly for the first time in your life. It can be extraordinary to watch ourselves turn into vengeful maniacs when we always thought we were so civilised and rational. Ultimately, Pluto transits help us to become more conscious of our wholeness, warts and all, and less likely to continue to project our darkness onto others or onto the world.

Audience: When I had my Pluto square I was travelling, and everywhere I went there was some kind of natural disaster. But it didn't feel weird, it felt it would be strange without it. Everywhere, just before or just after, had some kind of natural disaster, hurricanes or earthquakes, buildings falling down, people were dying. I was wading through it, but it felt quite normal. Now I think it was as if I was dragging that Pluto square around the world with me.

Neptune Transits
Neptune spends around 14 years in each sign, carrying the collective ideals and mystical yearnings of each successive generation. Neptune's house describes the area of life where we invest in our dreams. Neptune is always thirsty for perfection and beauty and magic and yet, like the myth of Tantalus, what we long for always seems to remain just out of reach because, ultimately, it does not belong to this world. Natal Neptune also indicates where we refuse to face reality, the part of us that does not want to be bothered, that does not want to struggle, that does not want to have to take responsibility. Neptune can be our ivory tower, where we are separated from, but dreaming about, life. Where we want our dreams to come true without having to do anything at all.

For as long as we seek to realise Neptune in a concrete sense, to gain something for our own personal gratification, we will deceive both ourselves and others, since Neptunian dreams are soul dreams, and don't belong to this three dimensional world of time/space. If we try to harness Neptune to our own ego purposes, then we remain fundamentally narcissistic, demanding that the world and other people adapt themselves to our perfect vision, and we will experience or perpetrate deception, chaos and false illusions.

For example, if we want something for ourselves where Neptune is, then one way of getting what we want is by becoming a victim or a martyr or a psychic vampire, which can be subtle but powerful ways of attempting to control others. The boundaries around who is doing what to whom are usually very hazy when we are talking about Neptune, which is why it can be so insidious and where we can poison ourselves and others. But Neptune also describes our capacity for unconditional compassion, devotion and service when it is not looking for any kind of personal return.

Audience: Would that be like having Neptune in the twelfth house?

Clare: Yes, and we could say that it describes a genuine mystical connection with the whole, because Neptune is our collective dream about accessing and returning to the source of life itself.

Neptune transits can also soften and loosen up natal patterns, bringing a magical dimension to our experiences, and we can become more sensitive to beauty in nature or in the arts, interested in music, dance, photography, film and all things magical and mysterious.

But Neptune transits can also dissolve our dreams, illusions and fantasies, and we can feel cast out, alone, rejected and abandoned by the gods who have spun the web for us until then. So these transits are often accompanied by an immense sense of loss and a period of mourning and grieving.

Around the age of 42 transiting Neptune squares our natal Neptune, and our ivory tower begins to dissolve. For some time now I have been working with a woman with Sun in Aries and Mars in Sagittarius opposite Jupiter, so she has a great deal of focus, optimism and enthusiasm. But she also has a Moon-Neptune conjunction in her chart, in Libra. Her experience of her mother is that she is extremely needy and dependent, not strong enough to stand on her own feet. This conjunction indicates a symbiotic relationship with mother, and it is very hard to cut the psychic umbilical cord, if not impossible. My client has projected her Moon-Neptune conjunction onto her mother, which allows her to remain consciously strong, independent, focussed and energetic. But we know that the Moon is always hungry and that Neptune is always thirsty, and this conjunction, which often indicates an addictive personality, had found another way to express itself in my client's life – she had been an alcoholic for many years.

As my client approached her Neptune square Neptune she began to feel increasingly depressed and found herself crying all the time as a great deal of grief began to well up. But because she had built up a strong, professional, optimistic and energetic persona, there was no place in her life for these feelings and she started taking antidepressants in order to be able to carry on with her busy life.

As an Aries Sun woman, she is goal oriented and as the Neptune square Neptune became more exact her instinct was to turn the headlights on and drive straight into the fog, which of course makes the fog denser. If you are a Piscean type then you are used to the fog and better able to navigate through it. But if you are used to being focused and driven, the Neptune experience can be excruciating, because you cannot think so clearly and can no longer see where you are going.

Audience: Has the relationship with her mother changed?

Clare: Well, it hasn't changed yet. We could say that the purpose of Neptune transits and particularly the Neptune square Neptune is to enable us to let something go, to grieve and mourn the loss of an illusion of protection. My client has been reluctant, or unable, to accept her own vulnerability and neediness. But underneath the depression I suspect there is a great deal of unconscious rage about the reciprocal collusion and manipulation which has bound her to her mother, and the personal sacrifices she has made as a result, and this would need to come to the surface before a healthy separation and eventual healing can take place.

Ultimately, one way for her to integrate these opposing themes might be for her to use the focus, courage and vision of her planets in fire in the service of the Moon-Neptune conjunction and devote herself to a collective cause, such as working for charities concerned with homelessness or displaced peoples. This would fulfil the competitive and crusading nature of her Sun and Jupiter as well as the devotional nature of her Moon-Neptune, and provide her with a wider field than just her personal relationship with her mother. As Jung so rightly observed, problems are never solved, but they can be outgrown.

Audience: When I had Neptune on my natal Sun, I was so depressed I felt I was ready to die. It didn't bother me that I felt that way, I wasn't suicidal, but I just didn't want to live any more. But I actually went on Prozac at that time, and that helped me to rediscover hope. And when I first started to learn about astrology, I was really interested to discover that Prozac is connected with Neptune.

Audience: I have Neptune in the first house and when I had my square I decided that there were many things I just did not believe in any more, and that I was going to do something completely different, which I did.

Clare: So, your Neptune square Neptune enabled the personal mists to clear and provided an opportunity for a different kind of self definition?

Audience: I had some weird experiences, which helped me to decide I was not going to be deceived or nebulous any more, and that felt really good.

Clare: Under Neptune transits our old gods die and we can lose our direction, which can be an intensely painful experience, heralding a period in the wilderness when everything seems meaningless and we feel lost and abandoned. This can feel unbearable, and of course we would much prefer not to surrender to the confusion, disillusion and grief as our false dreams, fantasies and longings are dissolved. But they are ready to be replaced by more appropriate ideals and eventually there will be new gods and dreams and ideals which will be better capable of sustaining us in the future.

Uranus Transists

Uranus transits bring new levels of awareness, insight and perspective which enable us to break old patterns and free ourselves from old habits which have become limiting or inappropriate. The question we might ask under a Uranus transit is: 'What old patterns or assumptions are no longer appropriate? Where do I need more autonomy and freedom?'

The natal placement of Uranus describes how a particular group of people born within a seven-year period will react against and break the old patterns of the sign in which Uranus is placed. Uranus in a sign is an example of a collective ideology whose time has come – a new way of thinking which is shared by a group of people. It is interesting that the same ideas often seem to emerge all over the world at the same time – like scientific breakthroughs, for example. This is an extremely Uranian phenomenon, and one which has been explored by Rupert Sheldrake in his theory of morphic resonance.

As always, we need to consider the sign of the natal Uranus. A shorthand approach to the collective meaning of Uranus would be to ask 'what inherited conventions don't we believe in?' So the Uranus in Cancer generation doesn't believe in the nuclear family and we could say that its function is to construct new tribes and clans based on shared ideals rather than shared genetics. The Uranus in Leo generation doesn't believe in privilege or entitlement and so its function is to forge a new recognition that every single person is special and unique in some way. The Uranus in Virgo generation doesn't believe in the old rituals of service and work, and its task is to forge new ways of working together, and so on. The inherited structures are not acceptable to Uranus, and some kind of new thinking is needed.

Let's look at the transits of Uranus and at its cycle. As always we have to start by examining the natal Uranus by sign, house and aspect, since different people will experience the transits of Uranus in different ways. Uranus transits bring radical, often unexpected, change – opportunities for new insight and understanding and the breaking of old patterns. Uranus is the shaker, it wakes us up. If you are Aquarian or Sagittarian then you are not going to find Uranus transits as difficult or threatening as an earthy Taurean, for example.

The Uranus cycle is 84 years long, with the waxing square occurring around the age of 21, at the same age as the first waning Saturn square Saturn. So the impulse for freedom and the fear of that impulse are present in equal measure. This is often the first realistic opportunity we have to make autonomous decisions and plans, to break away from the Saturn structures of our family and from family conventions and social expectations.

Audience: When I was 21 I went travelling round the world for a year.

Clare: Presumably that was not necessarily part of the family's plan for you? Was it expected and accepted that you would spend a year travelling?

Audience: Absolutely not, but it was something that I wanted to do.

Audience: My daughter was 21 last week and she suddenly split up with her boyfriend of 18 months. It was suddenly all over – and the new boyfriend has already moved in. Just like that – exactly on her 21st birthday.

Audience: That is interesting because I am having my Uranus opposition Uranus at the moment and so many of my friends have been telling me that they were going to split up with their partners or that their marriages were on the rocks. And I have been listening to them and supporting them with all this, and thinking how calm and peaceful my own life had been for the last few months. And then suddenly I split up with my own boyfriend and I absolutely didn't see that coming.

Clare: So it happened to you as well.

Audience: Yes, but all the time I have been wondering why we did that because there is nothing really wrong. But it just doesn't feel right any more. I was meant to be going on holiday with him next week, but I can't do it. And I don't really care about breaking up, which is really strange, because a year ago or so it would have been really terrible, but now it just feels right. It is like a complete flip.

Audience: My natal Uranus is in the seventh house, and when I was 21 I couldn't decide between two men, who both wanted to marry me. So I went travelling instead.

Clare: At the time of the Uranus opposition around the age of 42, the impulses we felt around the time of our Uranus square Uranus will be felt once again, with the added charge that we feel there must be more to life than this. We have the powerful urge to be true to that Uranian principle in our birth charts and ready to upset the existing apple cart.

And around the same time transiting Saturn has reached its opposition after the first return, so we will also be assessing the decisions we made at the Saturn return, and reaping the rewards of those decisions, or perhaps finding them wanting.

This is a time when people can and often do suddenly change course. If they have been paying tribute to Saturn, working hard, serving their families and achieving status in the eyes of the world, the temptation to throw all that away and reach for a new freedom which holds unknown possibilities may be very strong indeed. And equally this could be the time when a person who has always been a free spirit will put on a suit and tie and settle down – also a radical change.

Audience: I have Uranus in Cancer in the eighth house, and I gave up my well paid job in banking when I was 42. I really didn't care about money any more.

Clare: Uranus transits bring the kind of insight which cuts right through the old patterns and habits. We see things differently, we feel more detached, we can extract ourselves from aspects of our lives which make us feel trapped. And this can be quite uncompromising and very clear, not subject to discussion or debate.

Audience: I know what you mean. I finally ended a relationship quite suddenly. I had been trying to get out of it for seven years, and then all of a sudden I could do it, it just happened.

Clare: Of course it is equally possible that the Uranus transit will be experienced in projection, in which case unexpected events will happen to us. For example, if Uranus is transiting square the MC/IC axis there may be a restructuring at work which is nothing to do with us personally, but we might suddenly find ourselves redundant or doing a completely new job. This could well be the result of not acting on our own intuition that it was time to find another job. Instead, we hang on for the security, but then find that it happens to us anyway. So you can see how radical this cycle is. Why else would a perfectly rational, sensible person suddenly leave their family and job unless there was an immensely powerful desire for change, for more freedom and autonomy. Uranus transits rattle our cages, their purpose being to wake us up, so that we can take a detached look at what we are actually doing with our lives. If we are already living lives which give us plenty of freedom and autonomy, then the Uranus transit will not need to shatter our structures but can be used to create more space within those structures. The Uranus transit is only experienced as shocking if we are afraid of change, and holding on too tightly to what we already know.

The waning square in the Uranus cycle occurs around the age of 63, after the second Saturn return, when most people are free from the responsibilities of work and so on. This brings opportunities to finally do things we have always wanted to do.

Audience: I have a friend who is 84 and has just had his Uranus return. He is designing a square rigger for a youth organisation at the moment. He is really vibrant, and has had an amazing life, quite fascinating, although most of his old friends have now died. I suppose you could say that he is eccentric, which is a Uranian word, isn't it?

Clare: Perhaps that is the joy and freedom of completing an entire Uranus cycle. There is no need to bother about fitting in any more. Jung has written about the two phases in the life cycle. The first outwards phase is when we are learning and experiencing and relating to the outside world, building friends, career, home and family. And then we reach the turning point, the full Moon point, of our lives and there is a natural shift in direction which he called the enantiodromia. And this second phase is about getting to know ourselves, integrating those parts of ourselves which have been hidden or dormant in the previous phase and becoming completely who we are. And the major midlife transits, the Neptune square Neptune, Uranus opposite Uranus and Pluto square Pluto are significant events which can help us learn more about who we really are, in essence.

Chiron Transits

Let's have a quick look at the transits of Chiron. Chiron orbits between the old solar system, bounded by Saturn, and the newly discovered collective planets, Uranus, Neptune and Pluto. As such it is the bridge between the personal and transpersonal realms, belonging to neither. And so Chiron is about sitting in the uncomfortable space between, and ultimately that is its gift.

The Chiron return occurs between the ages of 49 and 51 years, but it has an extremely elliptical orbit, so the ages at which the waxing square, opposition and waning square occur vary greatly from one person to another.

Have a look at this diagram and chart, which shows that Chiron becomes an inner planet – in other words it passes inside the orbit of Saturn – when it is transiting between Leo and Sagittarius. This means that anyone born with Chiron in late Leo, Virgo, Libra, Scorpio or early Sagittarius will have Chiron as an inner planet, and it will be moving fast, transiting each of those signs in around two years. As Chiron moves

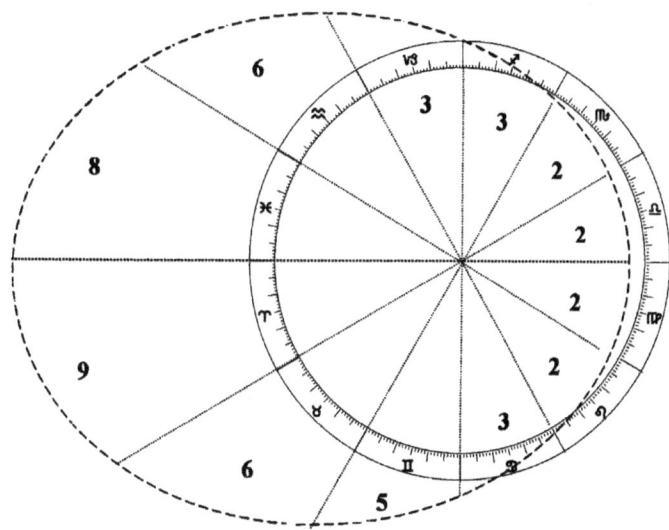

outside the orbit of Saturn again, its speed slows down considerably and it spends around six years in Aquarius, eight years in Pisces and nine years in Aries before beginning to speed up again.

Chiron transits carry the natal Chiron theme with them, and describe the journey which leads us from our first experiences of alienation, feeling rejected and misunderstood by others, to the discovery of our own inner values and the courage to live by them, whether or not they conform to the established social conventions.

The waxing square, opposition, waning square and conjunction all describe turning points in the Chiron cycle, and the approximate ages when these aspects occur are given in the table below. However, this is a very rough guide and the age can vary by plus or minus three years, so you will need to check the actual dates of your own Chiron cycle.

Natal Chiron	Waxing Square	Opposition	Waning Square	Return
	Encounter - alienation	Recognition - vocation	Understanding - compassion	Integration - acceptance
♈	12	23	30	50
♉	11	17	27	50
♊	8	14	28	50
♋	6	13	33	50
♌	5	16	37	50

Chiron becomes an inner planet in late degrees of Leo

♍	5	20	41	50
♎	7	26	43	50
♏	10	31	44	50

Chiron becomes an outer planet in late degrees of Sagittarius

♐	14	35	44	50
♑	19	36	42	50
♒	22	34	40	50
♓	21	29	35	50

The waxing square usually coincides with our first awareness of the natal Chiron theme in our chart, often through experiences of isolation or alienation. We can feel wounded – rejected, alone or inadequate in some way. This is often the time when the hero is constellated – we seek to deny or reject our own vulnerability and pain, and build strong defence structures around this painful place in our charts in an attempt to avoid a repetition of these feelings of alienation or inadequacy.

Sometimes we meet Chiron at the waxing square in the form of an illness which is later recognised as a kind of shamanic initiation. So we could say that the purpose of the waxing square is to single us out from the world, an experience which can change our life path.

At the opposition, this awareness of our difference can be recognised as a vocational calling, often connected with healing or teaching, but usually in areas which do not tend to be valued by mainstream conventions. The themes of the previous waxing square will once again emerge, and there is often some kind of healing crisis or breakthrough, and we might decide to learn more, or to train as a therapist, healer or teacher. At the waning square, when the themes of our natal Chiron emerge once again, we have the opportunity to let go of the feeling that we need to adapt, adjust or distort ourselves to gain acceptance in the eyes of others or of the world. We no longer need to try and 'fix' our supposed inadequacies and imperfections and have learned to accept ourselves and others just as we are through the development of true understanding and compassion. Ideally, the Chiron return brings with it a feeling of peace and personal authenticity. We are no longer bothered by the world's judgements and realise that our own painful experiences of alienation have actually become the source of our healing and teaching gifts, which can now be devoted to others. The Chiron return is associated with wisdom.

Audience: Can you say something about my own Chiron journey, Clare? I have a Chiron in Pisces opposite the Moon in Virgo.

Clare: So we know that Chiron was moving slowly when you were born, and your square would not have occurred until you were 21. It then began to speed up, and you had your opposition eight years later, when you were about 29, and your waxing square six years after that, when you were around 35. In your case, the Chiron cycle coincides with the significant Saturn transits, so you have no doubt felt particularly alone and unsupported at these points in your life. With Chiron opposite your Moon natally, the focus of your feelings of alienation and rejection will have to do with nurturing, with feeling safe and comfortable.

One helpful approach to the Chiron cycle is to think of it as a story about a pair of twins who become separated and then eventually reunited. These twins carry the opposites between them, light and dark, immortal and mortal, spirit and matter, intellect and instinct. The first Chiron square is often the time when the twins split, with one twin feeling unbearably hurt and the other side becoming heroic in the face of the pain. And of course we tend to identify with the heroic 'twin', and project the vulnerable 'twin' by investing a great deal of energy into nurturing everyone else and making sure they are cared for. But ultimately that doesn't work, because the suffering 'twin' within is even more abandoned and neglected than before.

Audience: That is exactly what happened because when I was 21 I became a nurse.

Clare: And no doubt you became an extremely efficient and dedicated nurse. But your vulnerable 'twin' was locked away so that nobody, not even yourself, knew it was there. And of course the problem is that we cannot be truly compassionate towards others unless we have first learned compassion for ourselves, and that is the Chiron problem. Pisces describes our sense of belonging to and being protected by the whole, the universe and the source of life itself. With Chiron in Pisces, when the split occurs it cuts us off from this deep sense of protection and belonging, and so we feel we have been cast out from the womb, as if the universal umbilical cord has been brutally severed. We feel particularly alone and have no alternative but to become heroic.

Audience: It seems strange now that I look back on my time as a nurse in intensive care. We were heroically fighting death all the time, and I was getting more and more exhausted. When I had my Chiron opposition I got really sick, and had a kind of breakdown which was really just complete exhaustion.

Clare: So the vulnerable, suffering, mortal side of yourself, the cut-off twin, which had been ignored all these years but which in fact holds the instinctive Chiron wisdom, came back into your life at the Chiron opposition and you were forced to reconnect to that part of yourself. Did you experience a vocational shift at that time, which would have emerged as a result of this illness?

Audience: Yes, that's right. When I recovered I started to train as a nutritionist, and of course I also started to eat the right things and to care for my own body, which felt like a much better way of helping people back to health. Actually, I had an interesting dream around the time of my illness. I went into a room where there was a band playing and they were all plugged into an amplifier. When I saw what was going on I went and got my lead and plugged it into the amplifier and started playing my ukulele.

Clare: So you reconnected to the source of the power – isn't that marvellous? Your psyche gave you a wonderful image during what was no doubt a shamanic illness, out of which emerged a vocation which no longer forced you to split, since it involved caring for yourself as well.

Audience: I can see that now, and in fact I am passionate about nutrition and about working with plants and herbs and potions. And I can see my clients benefit, so it is immensely rewarding. I have just realised that at my waning Chiron square I became a teacher at a school for nutrition, so that was another important part of my Chiron journey, and I really enjoy teaching too.

Clare: That is a really lovely example, thank you. I remember another, rather more disturbing, example of a student with a Moon-Chiron conjunction in the sixth house. He was clearly in the cut-off, heroic stage, denying any kind of emotional connectedness, and had decided that the only future for mankind was to leave the Earth and go and live in space – really. It was so clear to the rest of the class that the instinctual, animal side of himself had been dreadfully hurt, that nobody challenged this comment. When the animal side of ourselves has been really abused or damaged, then like a wounded animal we can't get too close or it will attack. So we can also be aggressive and defensive where our Chiron is, because we feel so vulnerable there. I sometimes think about this student and hope that the unfolding Chiron cycle has enabled him to make some kind of emotional reconnection.

Notes
1. Charles Harvey, *Astrological Journal*, March/April 1982.
2. Ibid.

LESSON 5

Transits of Saturn, Jupiter, Mars and the Inner Planets

SATURN AND JUPITER

As social planets, Saturn and Jupiter describe our relationship to the world and the way we engage with the social environment. The transits of Saturn and Jupiter are usually experienced as periods of contraction and expansion, pessimism and optimism, isolation and support. Both cycles bring opportunities for increased personal growth and maturity, encouraging us to build on past experiences and expand our horizons.

The table shows the average ages at which the hard aspects occur during the Saturn and Jupiter cycles, and you should be able to see the connection quite clearly. The hard aspects challenge the natal positions and make them more conscious. For example, at the age of six to seven, the first Saturn square and the first Jupiter opposition describe the first turning point in our relationship with the world around us. As we begin to experience these external demands, we are likely to feel resistance and fear, as well as excitement about our expanding horizons, in more or less equal measure.

The first return of Jupiter at the age of twelve, when our environment and horizons are usually growing educationally, is followed two years later by the opposition of Saturn, which coincides with puberty, when we often feel awkward and inadequate.

The first Saturn return coincides with a Jupiter opposition. On the one hand, we are assessing what we have, or have not, achieved during the first 29 years of our life, and making plans for the next cycle, and on the other hand we are likely to be questioning the goals we had at the age of 24, at the start of the second Jupiter cycle, and making adjustments, as different areas of life begin to hold new meaning for us. Let's have a look at these cycles in more detail.

Outer Planet Cycles Combined: Hard Aspects Only

Average Age	Jupiter	Saturn	Uranus	Neptune	Pluto
6-7	Opposition	Waxing Square			
12	1st Return				
14-15		Opposition			
18	Opposition				
21-22		Waning Square	Square		
24	2nd Return				
29-30	Opposition	Return			
36-37	3rd Return	Square			
36-38					Square (born 60s-80s)
41-42	Opposition		Opposition	Square	
44		Opposition			
41-46					Square (born 40s & 50s)
48	4th Return				
52		Square			
54	Opposition				
59	5th Return	2nd Return			
63			Square		
65	Opposition				
66		Square			
71	6th Return				
74		Opposition			
77	Opposition				
81		Square			
82				Opposition	
83	7th Return				
84			Return		
88		3rd Return			

Transits of Saturn

Clare: Let's start by asking some questions. What is the purpose of Saturn? What is its function? Why do we need Saturn in the chart and what would happen if it wasn't there? Then we can go on and look at Saturn's transits.

Audience: To learn about restriction and limitation.

Audience: Time to hold back, time to consolidate what we have learned.

Audience: To build foundations, to restructure and reground ourselves.

Audience: Time to cut away the fantasy and deal with the reality of life.

Clare: Absolutely. Saturn is, above all, the reality principle and its transits remind us that we have to function in the real world. And Saturn is to do with building solid structures and substance in our lives. Our normal rationalisations, avoidances and excuses do not serve us during Saturn transits.

There is no getting away from the fact that our first experience of Saturn is usually painful, since this is where we feel alone and isolated. Our early experiences will have made us vulnerable and sensitive in that area. So it is where we feel fearful and inadequate, it describes what we feel we have been denied, and what we therefore crave. The natural response is to build a strong defensive structure around this planet, usually in the form of denial or over-compensation. And because we are afraid, we tend to tense up, which often has the effect of reinforcing the original experience. We expect difficulty and isolation and so that is what we get. As early experiences of isolation or rejection are reinforced they begin to feel very concrete, as if that was our fate.

Audience: So this is where we feel stuck in inertia, or paralysed?

Clare: That's right. We tense up and contract where Saturn is in our charts and would remain frozen there if it wasn't for the transits, which repeatedly knock on the door, suggesting that we face our fears and engage with this great god of time and limitation. The seven-year cycle of squares and oppositions represents thresholds and rites of passage, which is particularly noticeable during the Saturn returns at the ages of 29 and 58, when the chickens come home to roost and we are faced with what we have actually achieved in the world in solid, concrete terms.

And it is natural at these times to feel a powerful urge to regress. We want to go back to what we knew, even if the previous position was frustrating and uncomfortable. When we are young Saturn is necessarily externalised, projected onto parents, onto authority figures, onto any kind of rules, laws or restrictions. We learn to obey, or to rebel, both infantile responses. The pay-off for taking this position is that we can continue to blame others – usually our parents or partners or our boss – for all the restrictions and frustrations in our lives. But, as lord of time, Saturn demands that we grow up, take responsibility for ourselves and become adults. So a tremendous tension is generated by the Saturn cycle. In spite of the fear, we are driven by life and by time to move onwards, to become more mature. Our task is to internalise the principle of Saturn and become our own law and our own judge.

The Saturn cycle – particularly the squares, oppositions and returns – reminds us that it is time to take responsibility for ourselves. You can do a quick exercise yourselves to find out what your relationship to Saturn is. Imagine that you are at a conference, during a tea break, and the speaker is about to resume but you have not finished your tea. There is a big notice on the door to the lecture theatre saying that tea cups must not be taken into the theatre. Do you automatically obey, do you decide to take your tea into the theatre because you want to finish drinking it, and return the cup after the lecture, or do you see the notice as a challenge – a rule which must be broken, and pour another cup of tea to take in with you?

Our instinctive reaction to being told what to do is revealing. In the first instance, we automatically obey the rule – Saturn is fully projected. In the second instance, we make our own decision based on the reality of the situation, working with, but not subject to, the rule. In the third instance, we rebel against the rule, taking a Uranian stance, which means that the rules apply to everyone else but not to us.

Audience: Do you think we normally project Saturn onto our partners?

Clare: Yes, I think that is very common, because the vast majority of committed relationships seem to be based on the Saturn-Moon parent-child dynamic, where one person takes the role of the parent, the authority and the law, and the other takes the role of the child, roles which are usually interchangeable. And an uncomfortable collusion is set up, which gives people an excuse not to do something because their partner doesn't like it. And that goes on until such time that one of those people wants to grow up and become an adult, which threatens the status quo, and all hell breaks loose. Unless the other person in the relationship is also open to change, the relationship will usually break up.

Audience: When you are talking about the Saturn transits, do you include the trines and sextiles as well as the hard aspects?

Clare: Yes, and the soft aspects will describe times when we can move forwards and consolidate or achieve something without feeling our usual levels of hesitation or fear. But, as I have said before, nobody ever visits an astrologer to talk about their trines and sextiles. When things are going smoothly we take them for granted.

Saturn rules time and during the hard aspects we tend to feel that time is running out. Our body usually obliges and, quite literally, we can physically age under a Saturn transit, and it is not unusual to experience some of the Saturn ailments, such as aching knees and bones, arthritis and problems with our back, teeth or skin. There is nothing like physical pain to remind us that we are mortal and getting older.

Audience: They say that Capricorns look younger as they get older. I have Saturn conjunct my Ascendant and I find that the older I get, the younger I feel. I used to be so much more rigid and fearful when I was young.

Clare: Yes, because you have been living with Saturn since you were born and have had no alternative but to engage with it. When we have come to terms with Saturn, learned its lessons and paid our dues, we are no longer afraid of its demands and we can begin to reap its remarkable rewards.

Audience: Well, not completely, but I am certainly not afraid of it any more.

Clare: So let's look at the major transits in the Saturn cycle, which occur roughly every seven years, at the squares, oppositions and conjunctions. For reasons I am not sure of, the applying periods seem to be the most painful and difficult. In the case of the Saturn returns, we seem to feel them most from about 18 months before the exact return.

Audience (Anne): I am interested in what you have said about regression. My daughter is coming up to seven and she wants to be very babyish at the moment. I have noticed that she has started chewing and sucking things and told her I was going to get her a dummy for her birthday.

Clare: This is the age when we have normally lost our baby teeth and are growing our adult teeth, which is, of course, symbolically significant. So that might explain why she is chewing everything at the moment. Is your daughter changing school?

Audience (Anne): Yes, she is moving from infant school to junior school.

Clare: A change of school often occurs around the age of seven, a time when both parents and teachers begin to expect more from children, and they feel that. The child's every painting is no longer greeted with rapture by its parents, there are increased demands and homework to be done.

Audience (Anne): This is really tough for her, but I know she cannot stay six forever.

Clare: Your daughter is on a Saturn threshold and part of her is afraid so she is regressing. It is one of the most painful things to watch your child of six, or 13, or 20 or at any hard Saturn aspect, become fearful, afraid and even depressed. And although, as parents, we can certainly provide a safe container at these times, we should not to try and rescue that child, although of course we would like to. But this is something they have to navigate alone, since that is the only way to build personal reserves and resources, which is the nature of Saturn. If your daughter can cross this Saturn threshold successfully, then she will have created an excellent template for all the Saturn transits to come.

If the transition is just too difficult and a period of regression is needed, it can manifest in the form of one of the 'transition' illnesses which are common at these times, particularly at the ages of 13 to 14, and 20 to 21, such as anorexia or glandular fever. Saturn is a hard taskmaster, laying down memories which are reawakened and evoked at each seven-year stage, which will need to be revisited and faced again.

Audience: So we remember all the Saturn transits and keep coming back to them?

Clare: Yes, and that is why Saturn feels like fate. If you have a client who is currently having a Saturn transit, it can be extremely useful to ask them what was going on in their lives at the ages of 14, or 21 or 29. Because the themes will repeat, and all the old fears will re-emerge. But as we mature, Saturn transits give us an opportunity to go back and engage with thresholds we were not able to cross before. To lay old ghosts. The particular nature of the old ghosts will be described by Saturn's natal sign, house and aspects.

Audience: That's interesting because I have Saturn in Sagittarius in the ninth house and I dropped out of university when I was 20, at the time of my waning Saturn square. Ever since then I was bugged by the feeling that I was not clever enough, that I couldn't do it. And this just wouldn't go away, so 28 years later, an exact Saturn cycle later, I actually went back to university and completed my degree. It feels really good at last to have faced that old devil and my feelings of educational inadequacy have dissipated.

Clare: That is an excellent example of the importance of the natal placement of Saturn, and you can be certain that those are the themes which will emerge. In forecasting work we always refer back to the natal chart. Every forecasting technique is an expression of the development of the natal chart. So it is never going to be the Saturn transit or the Saturn progression or the Saturn direction – its going to be my Saturn transit, and the function that Saturn will have for the rest of our life depends absolutely on its natal condition. So it is really important to go back when we are having a transit and analyse what it means in the natal chart.

So the challenges for you were to do with a higher learning and education story, and now that you have paid your dues to Saturn, the tangible rewards can be enjoyed.

Audience: Yes, because I am now training to be a teacher, which I could not have done unless I had got my degree.

Clare: Where Saturn is concerned, we need to pay our dues – to face our fears and work hard to achieve what we want. Working with Saturn's demands we build genuine confidence – 'this I have earned, and no-one can take it away from me'. When we have worked and achieved something, knowing it is ours by right is a great feeling. But of course Saturn takes a slow path, one step at a time.

Audience: What would happen to a child, a seven or six-year old, who didn't rise to the challenges of the Saturn square?

Clare: Well this could set up a pattern of feeling inadequate at school, socially or intellectually. The child might lose interest in her studies, because she doesn't feel able to keep up. But life goes on, and when the child reaches the Saturn opposition at the age of 13 or 14, the memory of the previous square will re-emerge, along with the experience of fear and resistance. And this can set up a cycle, or habit, of opting out. And, left to its own devices, this pattern may well be reinforced at the age of 29, 37, 42 and so on – until it is grasped and confronted.

Audience (Susan): My partner is seven years older than me, so we both have Saturn transits at the same time.

Clare: So we could say that this is a Saturn type relationship, the purpose of which is to learn from each other and to help each other grow up. It is not likely to be a barrel of laughs, but it can be mutually supportive, extremely enduring and rewarding over time.

Audience: So the personal meaning of the transit will depend on Saturn's natal sign, house and aspects?

Clare: That's right. With a natal Sun-Saturn conjunction, for example, the transits will involve the person's core identity and the Saturn journey will provide opportunities to take themselves seriously, building personal and tangible substance and authority.

Audience: My dad died last year, when transiting Saturn was on my Sun.

Clare: Saturn is the planet of manifestation and the transits of Saturn can be very concrete indeed. And the transits of Saturn carry memories, so it is possible that in seven years' time you may find yourself thinking about death or feeling afraid or worried about a male person in your life. But this may well have more to do with your father's death seven years before than with the current situation. Does that make sense?

Audience: Yes.

Clare: This is one of the great gifts of astrology, since it can help us to identify where feelings of fear, apprehension or inadequacy may originate and, if they are associated with the Saturn cycle, we can go back to what happened before and understand them better, since we are further along the spiral of time.

The first Saturn opposition occurs around the age of 14, at the same time as the Uranus sextile, so once again the fear of growing up is coupled with the urge for freedom and self expression. And it is not unusual for young people at this age to be rebelling at one moment, and clinging on the next. There is a great deal of social pressure at the Saturn opposition when young people are trying to come to terms with their changing bodies at puberty and often feeling inadequate and unlovable at the same time. Saturn brings isolation and we think we are the only person in the world who is not confident and popular. It is only later that we realise this is a universal experience.

The waning square of the first Saturn cycle occurs when we are about 21 years old, when we have usually completed our education and training and need to start earning a living, stand on our own feet and support ourselves. Or we might get married, which is another way of creating substance and structure. Now you are meant to be an adult. And once again there is likely to be fear on this threshold, wanting and not wanting to go forwards. We might decide to prolong our education and take another degree, or even succumb to an illness, such as glandular fever, which buys us time, because we don't feel ready for the world yet.

Audience: 21 used to be the age of voting and of officially becoming an adult. When you would be given the 'key to the door'. But there seems to be less and less safety out in the world. At one time you could get a job for life, but that has gone now.

Clare: That is an important point. All the old containers onto which we used to project our sense of safety, such as marriage, family, work, and social structures, seem to be breaking down. It is no longer so easy to find safe containers out there, so we need to become more personally resourceful, to build our own. That is something which is happening collectively.

The First Saturn Return
As we approach the Saturn return at the age of 29 we begin to realise that time is passing, that we are no longer able to be or do anything we want, that we no longer have infinite possibilities. This is normally a time when we reassess what we have achieved so far and start to make plans for the next cycle. And the memories of the previous Saturn transits will be reawakened. When I am working with clients at their Saturn return time, I always go back and explore the cycle with them, to see if there are any past experiences which might be getting in the way now, and this can be helpful. The Saturn return time can be experienced as a time of gaining control of one's life, achieving some kind of recognition and embracing adulthood.

Decisions made at the Saturn return will lay the foundations for the next cycle, and at the age of 35 or 36, at the waxing square, we can begin to see the results of these decisions. And that is another period of adjusting, will these decisions stand the test of time, are they still valid? And remember that Saturn is now back where it was at the first waxing square, when we were seven years old. Are there any memories from around that time? And then the Saturn opposition, the second time round, is at 42, and you reap the rewards of the decisions made at the Saturn return. And so the Saturn cycle is cumulative, and if you have not paid your dues to Saturn at the return, then you may regret the lack of solid achievement at the age of 42. Of course there is no law which says that we must face Saturn and learn his lessons, but we do know that they will keep knocking at the door.

Audience: I can remember my Saturn return quite well. I remember thinking on my 28th birthday 'you have to grow up now, what are you going to do with your life? Are you going for a career? Are you going to buy a home?' I can remember sitting and thinking that out, and then for the next few years doing it. And then at 36 I started to take my work more seriously on an inner level. At first it was just outwards, I did what was expected of me, but then I started to become more serious about what I did. I just felt that I didn't want to go on playing at it, and that has definitely reaped its rewards.

Audience: My friend did a research project recently on a homeopathic remedy which is associated with Saturn. What she noticed when she was taking their cases was that people coming to her at their second Saturn returns had had difficulties at their first Saturn returns which they had never resolved. There were particularly high instances of Parkinson's disease, or multiple sclerosis, all those kinds of illnesses where people are unable to move or go forward. And it is often the Saturn remedy which is indicated with those particular diseases. I think that is fascinating, because these patients often expressly referred back to something which had been unresolved when they were around 28 or 29.

Jupiter Transits
Jupiter has a 12-year cycle, which means that it spends around one year in each sign, and one year in each house if you use the Equal house system. Jupiter brings opportunity, expansion and optimism – even over-optimism – to the natal house being transited, since that is where we will be feeling supported and fortunate.

Audience: Does that mean Jupiter transits don't bring us luck?

Clare: In my experience we need to be rather cautious when it comes to interpreting Jupiter transits as lucky, since they can often give us a false sense of optimism, particularly if, as astrologers, we have any preconceptions about the inherent benevolence of this planet. Actually it is not that simple. Certainly, Jupiter is the great protector, but when we are under the influence of Jupiter we can be over-optimistic and unrealistic. Which is why a Jupiter transit is just as likely to blow up in our faces as to bring fortune and luck. The thing to remember is that Jupiter expands – so it will expand whatever it is transiting, according to the meaning of its natal placement.

So, for example, if we have a Jupiter-Saturn opposition in our natal charts, we will be prone to swinging between optimism and pessimism, expansion and contraction. Jupiter's transits will exacerbate this tendency, and we may feel extremely volatile and unstable for a while.

As always, the effects of a Jupiter transit depend very much on its natal story. I remember an example of a man who has a natal Jupiter square Saturn, so the Jupiter transits will bring the natal square with it. When transiting Jupiter was on his Moon his mother died and twelve years later, when Jupiter was on his Moon again, a relationship ended.

Audience: I remember when Jupiter was coming up to my Moon, and I was looking forward to travelling abroad, but in the end all that happened was that I got fat. [laughter]

Clare: Exactly. Or we might expect great riches and wealth when Jupiter transits the second house, but we simply become over extravagant instead.

Jupiter's transits expand the qualities of hope, optimism and faith which are described by the natal placement of Jupiter. Jupiter shows us the bigger picture, gives us the courage and faith to explore new realms. Jupiter's transits can reconnect us to our deeply-held beliefs and we sometimes get a sense that there is some kind of universal law or power greater than ourselves which is offering us new opportunities and encouraging us to go forwards. The shadow side of a Jupiter transit can be increased arrogance, ostentation and hubris. We usually feel restless under a Jupiter transit, and at its worst this can lead us into extravagant excess or unrealistic optimism, to the point of panic and mania.

So Jupiter transits are not always positive experiences, but the core meaning of our natal Jupiter will provide clues about the best way to co-operate with the fundamental development of this great protector in our lives, so that we use the transit wisely and it doesn't just burn itself up in over-optimism, chaos and disappointment.

Jupiter's transits through the houses bring opportunities and expansion in that area of life. For example, Jupiter's transit of the first house brings personal expansion, a renewed sense of self belief and an urge to explore. Jupiter transiting the second house can increase our feelings of self worth and bring in more money, along with the temptation to overspend. With Jupiter in the third house we might start a new course, find ourselves taking many more short journeys than usual, and see more of our siblings than usual. With Jupiter in the fourth house, the focus for expansion will be in the home and family. We may feel we need more space, and even build an extension. Jupiter in the fifth house is a time to enjoy our children, and to do something enjoyable for ourselves. With Jupiter transiting the sixth house our work might be going very well, or we might over-extend ourselves at work. With Jupiter in the seventh house, opportunities are likely to come to us through other people, and in the eighth house we could receive a legacy or other financial benefits. When Jupiter transits the ninth house we are likely to widen our horizons through long distance travel or higher education, and Jupiter in the tenth house will bring increased recognition. When Jupiter transits the eleventh house we might widen our circle of friends, and Jupiter in the twelfth house is a time of quiet development and making plans for the time when Jupiter returns to the first house.

At the time of the Jupiter return the adventures of the previous cycle have usually been fully explored and outgrown and we are ready to embark on a new cycle of expansion. This is the time to start a new venture. At the waxing square of the cycle, which occurs three years later, we will be challenged to commit to the new venture, and at the opposition, six years into each cycle, we have an opportunity to review the progress we have made so far and to make any adjustments necessary. And the waning square of the cycle, nine years after its beginning, brings further readjustments and the start of new ideas which will emerge during the next cycle.

Each Jupiter cycle carries its own intrinsic meaning, and it is fascinating how often our lives tend to broadly reflect these cycles of expansion and development. I hope this will become clearer as we go through this. The first cycle of anything is more or less unconscious; we have never met it before, it is a new experience. As the transiting planet goes round the chart for the first time, it sets a pattern which will be built on during subsequent cycles.

The second cycle, from 12 to 24, coincides for most of us with finding ourselves in a larger learning or educational environment. It ends with some kind of completion to our education, and even if we leave school at 15 we will still be doing an apprenticeship of some kind, gaining skills. By the age of 24, our basic education is completed. For some people, academics for instance, their next phase, from 24 to 36, will still be in education but at a higher level, perhaps as a lecturer. For most of us, this is when we expand into the world of work.

At the third return, which occurs around the significant age of 36, we are mature enough to be making a real contribution to the world and ready to start looking around at new possibilities, wondering what might be coming next. The fourth return occurs around the age of 47 or 48 and that is when we usually seek to bring more of ourselves into a new venture in the world. And the fifth return which occurs just after our second Saturn return, our challenge is to find something meaningful to live for, find a new faith in life and live by what we deeply believe in, now that we have embarked on our third Saturn cycle.

Now that we have looked at the Jupiter cycles in general terms, does anyone want to explore their own personal Jupiter cycles?

Audience (Sandra): Mine has always confused me, because it is in Capricorn and that seems like a contradiction.

Clare: This is a good example, because the question we need to ask is: 'What carries meaning for an earthy Jupiter and how does it expand?' In this case, growth needs to be tangible, taking place on the material, physical, plane. In Capricorn it can be about gaining professional recognition and respect. There is an interesting book by James Hillman called *The Soul's Code*, in which he writes about 'growing down', about becoming more earthed, about really incarnating.

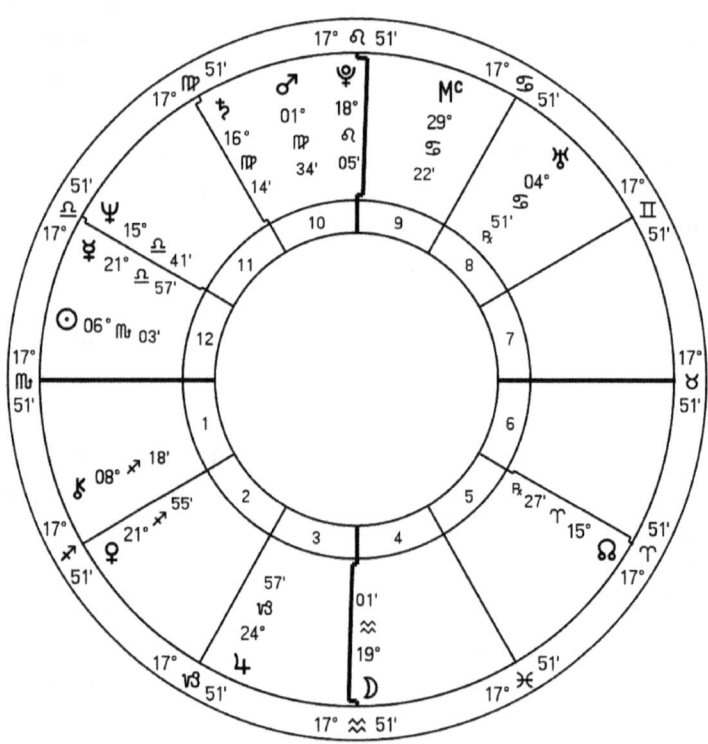

Sandra: Data withheld for purposes of confidentiality

Audience (Sandra): That really resonates with me. The need to get more deeply involved with the real world and with community, that kind of thing. And I know that everything of value that I have achieved has been the result of hard work. And I have learned that I have to be patient and that this all needs to be built slowly and gradually.

Clare: Capricorn's ruler is Saturn, lord of time. So for Jupiter in Capricorn there is something meaningful about time itself. So it might describe someone who is fascinated by time or by measurement, such as a cartographer or clock maker.

Audience (Sandra): Jupiter is in the third house, so it is also about communication.

Clare: Yes, and Jupiter in Capricorn in the third house indicates meaningful, practical communication. It is not just about gossip or anything lightweight.

Audience (Sandra): And this is tricky because it is square to Mercury in the twelfth house.

Clare: With Mercury in the twelfth house you need to catch the dreams, and use Jupiter in Capricorn to find a tangible expression for the imagination. Mercury rules the eighth house, so you will also want to find a way of writing with emotional depth. You will want to give form and structure – Capricorn – to your philosophy or your imagination or some kind of inner truth. And that is the challenge of the square, I think. Jupiter is also semi-square your first house Chiron, so you will want to write from your own personal experience, possibly about your search for faith, since Chiron is in Sagittarius.

Audience (Sandra): Does Chiron in the first house have anything to do with the body, and maybe the pain of incarnation?

Clare: Yes, for sure. You may feel an acute awareness of being imperfect or inadequate in some way.

Audience (Sandra): For most of my life I have been lost in an emotional quagmire, and struggling to get out of that into my real creative potential, where I can actually write and communicate something about that. But I have difficulty slowing my mind down enough to capture ideas, and find myself going on to the next stage and forgetting the stage before. In order to be able to write and teach you need to be able to capture the steps along the way. So I keep these elaborate journals to try to slow it down and capture it. I often feel that this book is an unachievable goal.

Clare: No, it is not. Not with Jupiter in the third in earthy Capricorn. It is not unachievable, but it will no doubt take time and patience.

Audience: I have a question. Do you find that these things you want to write about are just too big to capture, you do not know where to start and you want to have the whole thing in your mind before you put it down. Do you have that kind of feeling?

Audience (Sandra): That is part of it, but it is also that when I start writing, and I have several times, it just comes out preachy, and I hate that preachiness.

Clare: Well, they do say that Jupiter is where we play God. [laughter] Let's have a look at the transits, now that we have some sense of the meaning of Sandra's natal Jupiter. At the first Jupiter return around the age of twelve, we often change school, go to big school, and find ourselves in a wider educational environment. And we know from your third house Jupiter that learning and education carry meaning and significance for you.

Audience (Sandra): When I was 13 I actually left home and went to school. I asked my parents to send me to boarding school. I was born in a very small town and the school there wasn't very good. I also wanted to get away from my crazy family.

Clare: This is an excellent example. With Jupiter in the third house in Capricorn, a formal education is of value to you, and you needed to find the right environment so that you could develop beyond the

Transits of Saturn, Jupiter, Mars and the Inner Planets

existing system. This placement is educationally ambitious, and you wanted the kind of school where you could learn seriously and achieve the best grades. This is a very sensible and practical Jupiter. This change of school also meant you had to travel away from home, so you literally expanded your physical world and educational opportunities.

Audience (Sandra): It completely changed my life.

Clare: So now it would be very interesting to hear what the next cycle brought, when you were around 23 years old. Now that we know what happened at the start of your second cycle, we are much better informed to predict the major themes which might occur at the start of your third cycle. We can say with some confidence that this will involve a new vision which is the result of some serious strategic planning and which will involve a move into another geographical area.

Audience (Sandra): I finished graduate school when I was 23 and then I joined the Foreign Service. [laughter]

Clare: Perfect. And what was your motivation?

Audience (Sandra): I wanted to be paid to travel.

Clare: This is a wonderful example of a practical philosophy, to be paid to travel, and so the next chapter of expansion came through your work, which literally involved exploring the world. It would be fascinating to hear what new chapter opened up for you when you were around 36 and embarking on your fourth Jupiter cycle.

Audience (Sandra): Well, I left the Foreign Service when I was 30, which was the Jupiter opposition phase of that cycle. I went home to have my family. I had one child already and then two more. At 36 I had my last child and that is when I started learning homoeopathy and developing a career in health. So I was working in an entirely different environment.

Clare: So there was a major adjustment at the opposition phase of your fourth Jupiter cycle, at the age of 30, which of course coincides with the Saturn return.

Audience (Sandra): Yes, I left at the height of my career. Something really strong drew me back home, which I think was more to do with the Saturn cycle. But then at the age of 48, at the next Jupiter return, I opened my own healing centre. There was a lot of personal healing going on during that time, and I was working with a group of intuitive healers. It was also when my marriage ended.

Clare: Working with a group of intuitive healers and opening a healing centre is an excellent description of the twelfth house Mercury square Jupiter, and your own personal pain and healing is described by the first house Chiron semi-square Jupiter.

Audience (Sandra): And then soon after my 48th birthday I joined the Foreign Service again. I did some re-training and went right back out into the world, which came as a surprise to me, but I had spiritual guidance to do so, so I just did it. And now I have been sent to London.

Clare: That is most appropriate, because the fifth cycle is often a more spiritual cycle, and Capricorn is a spiritual sign, where we are asked to 'bend the knee' to a higher authority. With Jupiter in Capricorn, that is the source of your faith, being open to what is asked of you, even if you don't know why. The last time you had a Jupiter opposition you reached the culmination of your career in the Foreign Service and you left. Now that you are 53, it will be interesting to see what happens in three years when Jupiter is once again at opposition.

Audience (Sandra): I never really had any handle on my Jupiter before, this is really helpful.

Clare: This is an example of how working actively with the transits in our own lives can be an immensely creative process. Knowing about the Jupiter returns can really give us the confidence to connect back to

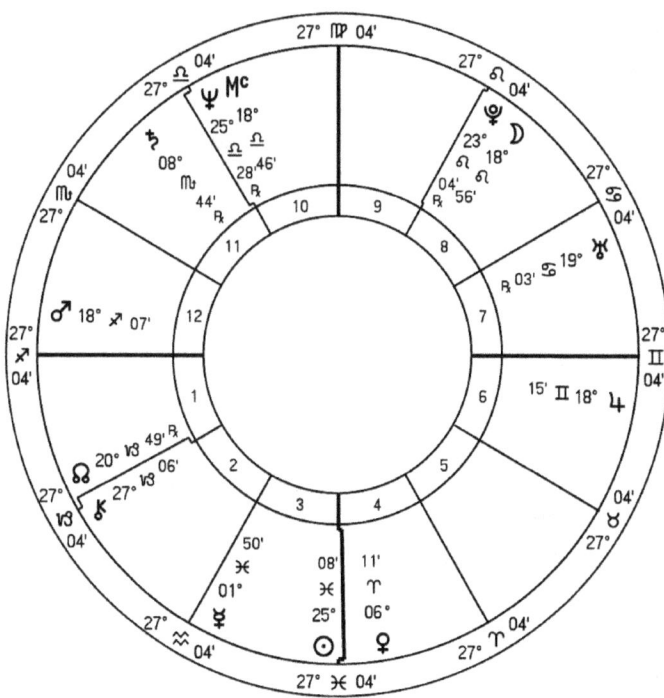

Sally: Data withheld for purposes of confidentiality

what is really meaningful for us in a core sense and to embark on a new chapter which will be an expression of that meaning.

Audience (Sally): My own life is a good example of excess, and I seem to have messed up all the stages, or done them backwards. I have Sagittarius rising, so Jupiter is my ruling planet. It is in Gemini in the sixth house of work and health, both of which have been terrible most of the time. Maybe that is because it is opposite Mars in the twelfth house. But it feels like my handicap place – where Saturn or Chiron should be, not Jupiter. I also have Neptune in Libra on the Midheaven.

Clare: Well, there is bound to be meaning in there somewhere, something important in those experiences which you may be judging, because they weren't necessarily how you would like them to be, but there is probably an important thread in there.

Audience (Sally): I hate those developmental stages in psychology books where they talk about 'when you are a mother' and 'when you get married' and so on. What if you don't do those things? When I first left America and came here, I met a psychotherapist who said I was 'age inappropriate' – like I did not live my life according to the right stages or whatever, like everything was backwards. As it happens, I am now 47 and my Jupiter return was two days ago, and I hope this will bring something positive.

I was very idealistic as a kid, and when I was 13 I started taking LSD and was planning to go and live in a commune or something. But I was raped when I was 19, which was my Moon-Pluto in the eighth house experience. That really shook me up and I got very depressed, started drinking and taking acid and stuff. Had that rape not occurred I think I might have become an artist, but then I started to get really angry and became quite self destructive. So I got derailed around the age of 19.

Clare: So your original plan was to be an artist, and you have Sun and Mercury in Pisces and Neptune conjunct the Midheaven in Libra, so that is a most appropriate ambition, although it can be difficult to be single-minded and focused on your career direction with that placement, and no doubt there have been times when you have lost your direction. What was going on for you when you were around the age of 23 or 24, at the second Jupiter return?

Audience (Sally): In my early 20s I went from being a hippy to being a punk rocker with attitude and wearing all black. First of all I wore only colourful things, and then I became really Plutonic. Everything was bleak and dark and I started doing heroin at 24. That must have been around the time when Pluto was transiting my Neptune and MC. And then I got hepatitis, which is Jupiter in the sixth, I guess. And then I got pregnant and had an abortion, though I didn't really want to, but my partner said I could not have a kid because I was so selfish. I felt really bad about that. And then a little bit after 24 I went into treatment and quit all the drugs. I got sick of all the people I was hanging around with, all taking drugs. So I moved to an area where there were really straight people living in the suburbs to get away from all the musicians and partying and drug-taking. I didn't have any friends at that time so

Transits of Saturn, Jupiter, Mars and the Inner Planets 89

I decided to make sense of my life by reading, and I went into a hermit stage where I hardly went out at all and just read books. And I studied all the things I am interested in now, occult things like the I Ching, and Jungian psychology.

Clare: That is an excellent example of the Jupiter in Gemini in the sixth house and Mars in Sagittarius in the twelfth house. So this was a hermit phase when you took yourself off into the twelfth house to read and learn. So the second Jupiter cycle was a destructive one but then at the age of 24 there were a series of crises which pulled you back and started you on a new journey of learning.

Audience (Sally): By the time I was 29 I was hiding away, not going anywhere, but a friend of mine was in a band and he really wanted me to go and hear him play, so I went. I hadn't had a boyfriend for a long time at that stage, I saw this guy from across the room and we really got along on an intellectual level. He was half American Indian so we both felt like outsiders. Six months later we got married, when I was 30, and then we had our own little house and did all the normal things.

Clare: So what happened when you were 36?

Audience (Sally): When I was 35 he committed suicide, and then I lost my home. I decided to give everything away and travel around the world on a vision quest, which I suppose is the Jupiter-Neptune trine. I felt America and I were not very suitable for each other. I had had enough and just wanted to get out of there. And now I guess that my new cycle which is just beginning is about coming here, to London. What I am hoping to do now is to develop my education because although I was always reading at home alone, I never finished any class. I have always started things and quit. I always had to work and trying to get to school, but my health wasn't very good, so school would get left out because I didn't have the energy to do both. And now I really want to stick with something, and I think that is the Saturn coming through now. I want to get an education and do something positive with all this Neptune and bring together all my interests, like coming to this class I suppose.

I went to a vocational counsellor where they make you check off all your interests, and I ticked about 20, so of course with Jupiter in Gemini I am interested in everything. For the last five or six years I have been working in a charity shop, which is also a Gemini thing. The pay is terrible but it is for a good cause. It's not what I want to do because there is no security for the future, but I feel comfortable for the moment. I would never want to do a job just for the prestige or money, I always had to have some kind of meaning in it in one way or another.

Clare: I think we can hear your Jupiter in Gemini in the sixth house very clearly in what you say. And also your Sun and Mercury in Pisces in the third house, both of which are also ruled by Jupiter. And so, Sally, what would you like this next cycle to be about, since you had your Jupiter return on Monday, two days ago?

Audience (Sally): First I have to quit smoking. I keep struggling with this one. Then I am going to start exercising because I want to keep my health as best as I can. And then I am going to save up for a computer, and I want to continue taking these classes. Eventually I would like to be self employed. And besides astrology I think I would like to take up gardening in the summer, which is sort of grounding. I would like to do lots of things. And I would also like to write, but I need a PC because I write everything long hand and my hands get tired. Those are my goals. And when I am older I would like to have a home and all the things I have lost, and look after some animals. I hope I will never stop learning, and I think it is all beginning to come together.

Clare: So in a sense you are now at the beginning of another vision quest, and you already know what you want the next twelve years to be about.

Audience (Sally): I am not afraid of my Pluto-Moon any more, of my darkness. I feel that is over with, and I am not afraid of the unknown. My only problems of late are practical ones: energy, time and money, trying to get those things sorted out.

Audience: Isn't that all sixth house stuff? Routine and work and how we earn our daily bread?

Audience (Sally): Yes, although unfortunately I don't earn as much daily bread as I would want.

Clare: I wonder if you might perhaps write all this down, make a commitment to yourself to follow your dreams at the beginning of this very important Jupiter cycle?

Audience (Sally): Actually, I have started to do that, looking at my whole chart and going back into my childhood dreams. And I have been decorating my flat and have made a garden on my little bed-sit roof. What I figured is that I would need Saturn, which I have always rejected, to help me stick to something and finish it, instead of abandoning it midway. I would like to say one thing before you move on. Having everything taken away from you so many times does give you faith because you realise that whatever happens you can survive, and you don't really need anything but yourself. I have had panic attacks before, but now I don't fear falling apart or anything, so I have an inner security and a strong inner faith that I did not have before, through these things happening. Whenever I have had bad times, even though I might have been actively self destructive due to depression, underneath it all I sort of thought there was a meaning anyway, at the back of my mind. And I always believed that I would not let it break me, and that I would bring myself back from the brink and not completely crash.

Clare: Thank you Sally. I think we have all been inspired by your story.

Transits of Mars and the Inner Planets

With the transits of Mars, Venus and Mercury we can really start to enjoy ourselves. As we have already seen, it is important to use the transits of the planets out to Saturn as actively and creatively as possible. We can learn to ride the waves of these transits, using them when the moment is right, and in so doing align ourselves with the 'will of the heavens'.

Mars is the planet of our personal potency, assertion and survival, so it is important to use the transits of Mars to serve our conscious goals.

Transiting Mars acts as a trigger, focusing on particular points of the chart in its two-year cycle, and if we harness that energy as it transits around the chart, we will feel increasingly confident and empowered. The first Mars return occurs at the age of two, known of course as the 'terrible twos', when the child is developing its own will.

Audience: That's when you learn the word 'no', isn't it?

Clare: Yes, and it is interesting to think back to how well that was handled by our parents. How did they react to our first attempts at independence and assertiveness? And we can normally tell this from the birth chart. If, for example, we have a Mars-Neptune aspect, then it is possible that our parents were unable to cope with our direct demands or expressions of anger. And so we would have learned a very subtle way of getting what we want, because it was not acceptable to use our Mars in an overt way. With a natal Sun trine Mars aspect, on the other hand, we may well have gained recognition by asserting ourselves, or by being athletic and competitive. With a Saturn-Mars aspect the message may well be: 'If I assert myself I will be blocked or criticised'. A Moon-Mars aspect is emotionally volatile. If it is in a trine, then it is likely that our family is emotionally highly charged, and it would be normal and unthreatening to express our feelings. Indeed, we might even need a good fight in order to feel safe. If it is in an opposition, however, then we might feel we have to fight to get our needs met. It is the natal Mars story which will be repeatedly constellated as it transits around the chart every two years.

Audience: I know exactly what you mean. I have Mars square Mercury in my chart and I really enjoy a good debate or argument – it makes me feel strong and clear. But my sister phoned me the other day and something she said made me feel very angry, although I didn't mention it at the time. So I had all this undischarged energy and dropped a laptop I was carrying onto my toe, which I thought was a good example of Mars square Mercury. [laughter]

Clare: That is a very good point, because Mars energy needs to be discharged. The question is whether our anger and assertiveness can be cleanly expressed and therefore used up, or whether it gets bottled up, in which case we are likely to attract arguments or accidents, which will have the effect of discharging that blocked up energy for us. If there is a problem with the clear and direct assertion of Mars then it will find another way to express itself, either covertly, through projection or, in the worst case scenario it turns inwards and becomes aggression against oneself, or one's body. So it is important to reclaim our Mars and use it outwards in the world.

Audience: It is interesting how horrified people are when you assert yourself. It is as if we are meant to take whatever we are given.

Clare: I think people are afraid of anger to the extent that they are unable to assert themselves or express their own anger. The Mars cycle is also a cycle of passion and libido, and many people are aware of a two-year cycle in their relationships. If a relationship is alive and vibrant, it will be constantly changing and evolving. Every two years it will need to be refocused and re-stimulated for the next cycle. The Mars transits will give us clues about how and when to use our Mars energy.

Audience: I wonder what Mars was doing last week, because I saw two accidents and on Sunday night there was a fight in the street outside my flat.

Clare: Have you got anything in Pisces?

Audience: My Descendant is in Pisces.

Clare: So Mars was no doubt transiting your Descendant, which means that accidents are happening out there, in your environment. Taking this further, I might start wondering if you are feeling angry with your partner at the moment. With Mars transiting your Descendant in Pisces, it may well be that you are feeling taken for granted or manipulated in some way. So the accidents and arguments you witnessed are the projected expression of your own anger.

Audience: Bingo.

Clare: I remember a session I had a few years ago with a woman who had Mars in Gemini, so I was expecting her to be articulate and verbally assertive, even competitive. But when she arrived she was virtually mute and just listened passively to what I was saying. But just before she arrived the local council turned up outside my house to dig up the road, and we had to contend with a road block and the deafening noise of the drills. Afterwards I wondered if this was an example of the gestalt of her life, that wherever she goes she meets all the aggression, drills and noise which she is not doing herself. These are the kinds of experiences which happen all the time in astrology and which add to its magic. It is as if our charts are the atmosphere we carry around with us all the time, and they are manifesting all the time, either consciously or unconsciously, in projection.

Audience: Following on from this conversation, something happened to my 16 year-old son yesterday. He came home and told me he had hit someone, which is completely uncharacteristic. He does have a natal Mars-Uranus opposition but he is normally very disciplined and slow to anger, and does karate which is all about the controlled use of energy. He was quite ashamed of himself.

Clare: It sounds as if this Mars-Uranus was triggered, and in fact the Moon would have been on his Mars in Pisces yesterday, so perhaps he was already getting annoyed?

Audience: Well that is interesting because I was cooking yesterday and he came in pestering and looking in the saucepans, pushing more than usual.

Clare: So he was looking for an outlet, and this had to do with the Moon, which rules both food and mother?

Audience: So perhaps if he had had a row with me then he wouldn't have ended up hitting the other bloke?

Clare: Yes, that's possible, because he was looking for an emotional outlet, with transiting Moon triggering his Mars-Uranus opposition.

We will be looking at the cycles of the Sun and Moon during the next two weeks, but the approach we have been using with Mars transits also applies to the transits of Venus and Mercury, which usually move very fast, being on a degree for only a day or so. These transits can still be used actively and constructively. For example we might give ourselves a treat when Venus is on the Moon, or phone a friend when Mercury is transiting Uranus. And when they are in their retrograde phase, then we can take the time to spend on ourselves, in the case of Venus, or to catch up with our paperwork and reading, in the case of Mercury. It can be really useful to do this, not to mention great fun, to engage actively with and actually use the transits of the inner planets.

LESSON 6

Planetary Returns

Solar Returns

We know that the Sun transits around the whole chart every year, and each year there will be a moment when it returns to exactly the same degree and minute as the natal Sun. This can occur on the birth date, or on the day before or after, and this is your astrological birthday. The chart drawn up for that moment is known as the solar return.

The solar return chart sets the scene for the year ahead, so it can be read as an annual forecast. This technique has been used for thousands of years, and we know it was used by Kepler, who would cast his own solar return horoscope each year. Solar return charts were also popular in the 17th century, and William Lilly has a very useful and practical chapter on revolutions in his book *Christian Astrology*. He explains exactly how to calculate a return chart, and then he gives an example of a solar return, looking at the relationship between the natal chart and the return chart.

Now, every time a planet returns to its exact natal position, it is plugged back into its source, and re-energised for the next cycle, so it's a kind of recharging point, setting the scene for the next cycle. So it's a frozen transit, which has a real energy of its own for the period of the cycle. And this applies to all planetary returns, although it is the solar return which is most commonly used.

Like everything else in astrology, solar returns shouldn't work, but they do, and very powerfully too. However, as psychological astrologers, I think we need to find a new approach to them, and that's what I want to explore with you this evening. I think we can approach these charts not as telling us what will happen in the next year, but as charts which give us clues about what we should be doing during the next twelve months. In this way, we could think of solar return charts as encouraging us to act in certain ways and focus on certain themes and areas of our lives for the following year. That would be a way of working dynamically, in an active dialogue with the planetary gods.

There are two things we need to do when we are studying solar returns. The first is to analyse the solar return chart itself, looking for the main themes and keeping our interpretation very simple. And the second is to compare the solar return chart to the natal chart, since it is in fact a frozen transit chart, which remains relevant for an entire year.

The Sun has to do with vitality and the life force, with the development of our identity, personal authenticity and power. So the questions to ask the solar return chart would be along the lines of: 'How do I regenerate myself this year? Where should I put the emphasis and focus this year? What do I need to bring consciously into my life? What kinds of struggles will I need to engage with to express my identity, individuality and creative potential? Where is the heart energy?' The more we understand the solar return chart themes, the more we can cooperate in the process. It is as if the chart is saying: 'This is the map for the year – embrace it!' And this can be very helpful in client work, because it tells us what to encourage our clients to focus on during that year.

Audience: I think that's a valuable insight. I don't have any air in my natal chart but my next solar return chart has a strong emphasis in air, so I am wondering how to cope with that.

Clare: So you have an opportunity to gain perspective this year, a chance to look at things from a different perspective. It is up to us to choose whether or not to actively engage with the themes.

Audience: There seems to be something in human nature which is very resistant to change.

Clare: That's right. And so there is an element of challenge in the solar return chart. It is as if it was saying: You can choose to embrace this chart and use it actively and consciously, or you can let it happen to you.' This approach is no different, really, from our approach to the natal chart, but in this case the picture lasts for just one year. And, as with all annual cycles, we have six months to explore and develop the solar return themes, at which point the cycle will have reached its culmination at the opposition – the maximum point of objectivity. As the cycle wanes, we have more knowledge and maturity, and we can reap the benefits of what has been gained during the six month waxing period. Gradually, of course, the relevance of the solar return chart lessens as the energy for the next solar return gathers itself, although still in gestation. So I think it's a good idea to start looking at the next solar return about three months before it occurs, so that we can start thinking about the themes for the next year and prepare for them.

Audience: Last year, when I saw a Moon-Saturn conjunction in the twelfth house, I decided not to go there at all, but just to indulge the Sun and Venus in the ninth house.

Clare: And did you succeed?

Audience: To some extent, yes. Although my therapist is sick and tired of it. [laughter]

Clare: So it seems as if the Moon-Saturn conjunction has been expressed anyway in your therapy sessions, where no doubt you were doing the required emotional work, locked away in the twelfth house with your therapist – a professional woman working in private – very Moon-Saturn in the twelfth house.

Let's look at the approach to interpreting solar return charts, and I suggest you keep it really simple, looking for the major themes only. Firstly, it is always worth checking the general shape and balance of the chart. If the element balance is more or less the same as our natal chart, then we won't notice a difference, but some years the element balance will provide real clues. And the same is true of the modalities. Say, for example, that you are natally fixed, used to taking your time, seeing things through and making them work, moving quite slowly and only making changes when you are absolutely sure, and then you have a solar return with no fixed planets, but with the emphasis on planets in cardinal signs, then the chart is encouraging us to find a new goal, take on a new challenge and move forwards. And we can work with that and say to ourselves: 'Right, this year I've got permission to be cardinal, so I am going to embark on a new venture', something which fixed planets generally resist. Or if we are basically introverted, with most of our planets under the horizon, and our solar return has most of the planets above the horizon, then we are being encouraged to go out into the world and be more extroverted that year. Otherwise, there might be so much going on in the outer world that we actually shrink even further down into our comfort zone, and miss the opportunity to explore what might be going on above the horizon that year. It is up to us to decide how to engage with these charts.

Secondly, we need to pay attention to the house in which the Sun falls, which is the area of focus for the year. And the two inferior planets, Mercury and Venus, are likely to be in the same house as the Sun, or in one of the adjacent houses. So they serve consciousness, and the question is whether they are supporting the Sun this year, or not. Mercury describes our conscious thinking for the year, how we will be processing information, and Venus describes our values, pleasures and joys for the year. And if a planet is retrograde in the solar return chart then that is also significant.

Audience: Is that just Mercury and Venus or all the planets?

Clare: The further out a planet is, the more likely it is to be retrograde at the time of the solar return, so we should pay most attention to Mercury and Venus, which serve the Sun. Mars, Jupiter and Saturn deserve their own return charts, so we would look at these to get a better understanding of their current themes.

As I said, the major focus of attention in the solar return chart is the house in which the Sun falls. If we ignore it, then we will still be forced to attend to it. So, say the Sun is in the sixth house, then the chart is telling us to focus on our diet, exercise, health, working routine and generally getting our house in order. If we choose to ignore this, then we may find this is a particularly chaotic year, or we can get exhausted or sick, in which case our attention will still be drawn to sixth house matters, but negatively. So, the placement of our solar return Sun tells us where our focus should and will be for the year, for better or worse.

The angles and angular planets suggest how we should be expressing the solar principle in the world. As far as the aspects are concerned, I suggest you use small orbs, the same ones Rob Hand uses for composite charts. He suggests 5° for conjunctions, oppositions, squares and trines,

2° for sextiles and 1° for the minor aspects – the inconjunct, semi-sextile, semi-square and sesqui-quadrate. This gives us a simpler, stronger chart, which helps us to identify clearly the main themes for the year. And aspect patterns using these smaller orbs will give us the main story for the year.

Audience: Is there a pattern with these solar return charts?

Clare: Yes, there is a rough pattern, although it depends on the house system you use and I am not sure if it is particularly helpful. Roughly speaking, the Sun moves three houses clockwise, or backwards, every year. So if it is in the tenth house in the first year, it will be in the seventh, fourth, and first houses in the following three solar return charts.

Audience: So we get to experience all the houses, which is great.

Clare: Yes, although people travel so widely these days that the pattern can be obscured.

Audience: My solar return for this year set for my birth place has a Scorpio Ascendant, but if I set it for London then the Ascendant is in Sagittarius.

Clare: Well, if you are living in London at the moment, then the chart should be set for London. The point here is that the moment of time is fixed – it is the exact time the planet returns to its natal position. But the angles will change if the location changes. Every chart is in fact a global chart, and this is a feature of astro-geography and astrological relocation techniques. You can explore this further by reading a good book on astro*carto*graphy.

This means that, once you have the exact moment of the solar return at your place of birth, you can travel around the world meeting that same chart again and again, but with different angles, as the place changes. And when any planets in the chart come to the angles, then we will meet those planets in those places – they will take on a particular prominence. So if you are living in London at the moment, then the chart cast for London will describe how you relate to the world from London during that year, but that will only be true when you are in London. And if you were travelling a lot during a year, then you would keep relocating your chart to see what parts of the chart come into prominence when you are in a particular place. Some people even try to manipulate their solar returns and choose their angles by travelling to certain places for their birthday. I remember a student telling me that he had specifically travelled to Athens for his birthday so that he could get Venus on his solar return Ascendant.

Audience: So the idea is that if you have a planet rising in a certain place in the world, then that is what you will encounter there?

Clare: That's right. So if, for example, you decide that it is time to gain some public recognition during the next year, what planet might you want on your Midheaven?

Audience: Sun and Jupiter.

Clare: So, using relocation astrology you would find out where in the world either the Sun or Jupiter would fall on your solar return Midheaven, and that's where you would go, assuming it's not in the middle of the Pacific. In which case you're not going to get recognition next year, unless you row across the Pacific and drown, in which case you will probably hit the headlines. [Laughter]

Audience: So you are saying that we use the relocated chart for solar returns?

Clare: Yes, and so if we see Jupiter on the Midheaven running through Helsinki on our astro-geography map, then the next step is to cast the solar return chart relocated to Helsinki, to get the whole picture.

Audience: But if your student travelled specifically to Athens to get Venus on his solar return Ascendant, then presumably he would have to stay in Athens for long enough in order to experience that, because it won't be on his Ascendant anywhere else?

Clare: Exactly, and that is the flaw of this particular attempt to manipulate the universe to suit ourselves.

Audience: If your solar arc Sun is in the sixth house, can you avoid that by relocating, or is it somehow destined anyway?

Clare: Well that is a big question. Our particular culture is devoted to using the will in the service of the ego, to get what we want, or what we think we want. But when we are working psychologically with astrology, it might be better to engage creatively with the pattern for the year, just where we happen to be at the time.

Audience: Like the Wheel of Fortune in the tarot. Surely we should be working creatively with what comes up, rather than trying to avoid it?

Clare: Exactly, either we trust that or we try and control it. The question is whether we really want to deny ourselves the opportunity to engage with our destiny. After all, we are already the expression of, and subject to, the time and place where we were born, so that is a good question.

Going back to these patterns, and assuming that you stay in your birth place, the Midheaven will move anti-clockwise, or forwards, three signs each year. There is a 33-year solar return cycle of the Midheaven, so when we get to the age of 33, the solar return chart will have the same angles as your natal chart. So, say your solar return Midheaven is 12° Cancer one year, then it might be 11° Libra the next year and, say, 10° Capricorn the following year. This means that your Midheaven will be in the same mode for eleven years – cardinal, then fixed and then mutable, returning to cardinal again 33 years later. It is this phenomenon which causes the solar arc Sun to move backwards three houses every year.

And the Moon is in a dance with the Sun at the same time, moving clockwise, or backwards, through the chart, one or two houses a year. The Moon in a solar return chart indicates where our feelings will be invested and where they will change during the year. And that is exactly how it should be, really, with the Sun and Moon going in different directions, the Sun going forwards into consciousness and the Moon going backwards, processing and digesting, dreaming and feeling.

All the other planets in sequential solar return charts move clockwise – except for Mars, which has a radically different pattern, and which is why I think he needs his own return chart.

The Moon in a solar return chart is important, indicating, by sign and house, how we will be feeling that year and where changes will occur, since there is a kind of restlessness about the Moon in the solar return chart. The Moon has an eight year journey around the solar return charts, returning to the same sign every 19 years. And when you get a new Moon, or a Sun-Moon conjunction in the same house, or even better, an eclipse, then that is going to be a very significant year. A new beginning.

Venus has an eight year cycle, so there are only eight possible placements for Venus in the solar return chart. Isn't that interesting? Every nine years the Venus cycle begins to repeat itself, within about a degree, describing our values and pleasures, what we should be reaching out for that year.

Audience: Clare did you work out these patterns by looking at your chart from year to year, or are they in a book somewhere?

Clare: You will find them in the books on returns, which are on the reading list.

Audience: Do you do your return charts by hand, Clare?

Clare: Not any more, although when I was learning astrology we were taught to calculate them manually, and it used to take us a whole day to calculate one solar return chart.

Another reason for focusing mainly on the inner planets in solar return charts is that you will have already picked up the significant transits of the outer planets when you are interpreting the transits. For example, if you have Pluto transiting opposite your Sun then that is a major transit which will be around for several years. Nevertheless, noting which houses carry this opposition for the year might give us more perspective – a way of exploring the transit from a different angle.

Finally, it is worth pointing out that we can use timing techniques with these solar return charts. For example, we can follow the Sun's transit around a solar return chart at one degree a day, noting when it makes a conjunction to the planets and angles in the solar return chart. That can be quite a significant timing technique, bringing consciousness to the planets and angles. For example, when the Sun comes to conjunct the solar return Mars, it will bring focus to that Mars, and that would be a good day to get something done, to use the energy of the Mars and to achieve something. Otherwise it might just blow up into an argument. And when it comes to conjunct the solar return Saturn we might use that day to work hard or to achieve something, or even to wait.

Audience: That reminds me of my kitchen timer.

Clare: Yes, that's a great image, with the Sun ticking around the chart at one degree a day, telling us where our focus should be.

Audience: I have a Sun-Uranus conjunction in my solar return chart, with the Sun at 22° and Uranus at 26°, so does that mean that the Sun will conjunct Uranus four days later?

Clare: Yes, exactly. Once you've got your solar return chart, it behaves like a normal chart, subject to planetary transits.
 The other useful timing technique is to progress the solar return Moon at the rate of one degree a month, which means that it will only move about 12° or 13° during the year, but that might be significant.

Audience: I don't think I understand what you mean?

Clare: We will be looking at progressions later on this term, so this will become clear. The third timing technique is to look for any planets which will transit the solar return chart angles; because these angles describe how we will be relating to the world during the year, and planets transiting these points will activate our engagement with the world, according to the nature of the transiting planet. For example, it is worth looking to see if any of the planets in the solar return twelfth house will stay there for the whole year, or escape by transiting over the Ascendant and moving into the first house. So there are three main timing techniques for the solar return chart: the Sun moving at just over one degree a day around the whole chart in a year, the progressed Moon moving about 12 or 13 degrees during the year, and any transiting planets which might go over the angles of the solar return chart.

Audience: Would you always have a look at the solar return when you are doing a chart for someone?

Clare: Yes, I always do this for my clients in order to understand where their focus should be for the year. I thought it might be helpful just to run through some key words and ideas for the solar return Sun in the houses.

There is a kind of challenge or command in the house where the solar return Sun falls. So, with the Sun in the first house the command is to be more self-centred, have a kind of healthy focus on yourself and to be less concerned with what others think. This is a year for self discovery, time for a fresh start. So you have permission to be more independent and to put yourself first. This is a year of new beginnings, and you might start with the way you look, throw away your clothes and start again – something like that. With the Sun in the second house it is time to focus on your values and on your talents. So the question is, do you earn enough? Are you properly valued? And are you earning your money doing something you value and which enhances your sense of self? It is time to focus on these questions.

Audience: Does it also include knowing what gives you pleasure and being able to find beauty?

Clare: Yes it does, because the second house is about valuing yourself, doing what is necessary to feel good about yourself.

With the Sun in the third house, the focus is on communication and the challenge is to find something that stimulates your mind. Do you need to take a course, spend more time with your brother or sister or buy a new car? With the Sun in the fourth house, then the focus should be on your roots or on your home, wherever you feel you truly belong. Your attention should be drawn down and inwards as you focus on your deepest needs and feelings. It is a year when memories or events from the past need to be processed, a year to discover your inner strength. And an opportunity to define yourself both in relation to, and distinct from, your family.

With the Sun in the fifth house it is an important year for self expression and personal fulfilment. There is something spontaneous about the Sun in the fifth, a drive to have fun, to be the centre of your own life. To question whether you are actually giving yourself enough time and space for self expression and regeneration. This is a year to come alive, and possibly to take risks. It can indicate a love affair or something which opens your heart. A year to focus on children, or to release the inner child. With the Sun in the sixth house, this is the year to question whether your daily and working life serves you or whether you serve it. Can you express yourself properly at work or are you just trapped on a treadmill? Because the wrong kind of lifestyle creates tension and stress, which eventually causes illness. So the challenge this year is to reorganise your life in such a way that it's more manageable and more efficient. And to take care of yourself, look after yourself. With the Sun in the seventh house the question is how much of yourself are you giving away to others, because if you are too dependent on your relationship that does not serve your own personal growth. Alternatively, are you putting the necessary energy into your relationships? Dynamic and creative exchanges with other people, both personal and business partners, are the focus of the year. This is the year to gain new perspectives about ourselves through relationships.

The eighth house is the house of crisis, heralding the end of one phase of life and the beginning of a new phase, so it's a real turning point. This is a year when the direction of our life can change quite radically, and that can mean some kind of crisis, since there is no rebirth without the collapse of the previous phase. So it's uncompromising, a year to make decisions from which there's no turning back. We are forced to go into the unknown, to dig deep within ourselves to find a deeper truth and the strength to change. We are not meant to be sociable in the years when the Sun is in the water houses. These are private houses, the years when our energy goes within and we are rediscovering ourselves, or discovering aspects of ourselves for the first time. So when the Sun is in the eighth house we will be feeling very private.

Audience: And the eighth house is the house of inheritance, so is this also the year when you might have to deal with family demons and family secrets and taboos, and skeletons in the closet?

Clare: Yes, it can also be a year when we are dealing with death and inheritances, when old, long suppressed and highly charged emotions, often to do with family matters, come to the surface. And our sexuality can be heightened, bringing with it the usual eighth house themes – obsession, jealousy and possessiveness. It's not a year for living on the surface and we should not try to skate through this year, but to engage emotionally with what is emerging.

With the Sun in the ninth house we should be increasing our awareness, getting a sense of how we fit into the wider scheme of things. New areas of life are opening up and our perspective will change as a result. We need to live this year by what we really believe in, and have the faith and confidence to trust our own intuition and judgement. With the Sun in the tenth house we should be focused on our identity or place in the world. Our public image and the wish to be recognised is more important than usual. And there is often a change in the way you see yourself and in how you are perceived by others. This is the year to make a change in your social status, embark on a new job, perhaps, or a new direction in your career. The focus will be on the outside world and on how best we can contribute to public life.

With the Sun in the eleventh house, the challenge is to get involved with, or connected to, a group endeavour so this is the year to seek out the company of people who share your ideals and hopes for the future. It's a time of connecting to like-minded people and being drawn to working with a group of people in some kind of cooperative effort. And to discover what personal talents you have to offer to the group. Your focus for the year should be on friends and colleagues who value you for who you are. And with the Sun in the twelfth house you need more solitude, to retreat from the world to some extent and give yourself more time to be more inward-looking and contemplative. This can be either a year of feeling cut off and alone or, more positively, it can be used as a year to listen to your dreams and to draw inspiration and support from poetry, and dance, and music, and meditation. It is the end of a cycle, so it's a time of letting go and, perhaps, a time to mourn the past. It can also be a time when the past catches up with you and you meet the results of your own actions, so that you can clear the ground for the next cycle.

Audience: Like the Judgement card in the tarot.

Clare: Yes, that's right. Would anybody like to offer their own solar return? It would be good to look at a real live example.

Audience (Carole): Could you have a look at mine? Although I use the Placidus house system.

Clare: That's good, so it will give us some practice using Placidus. You were born in Argentina, but you are now living in London. How long have you been in London?

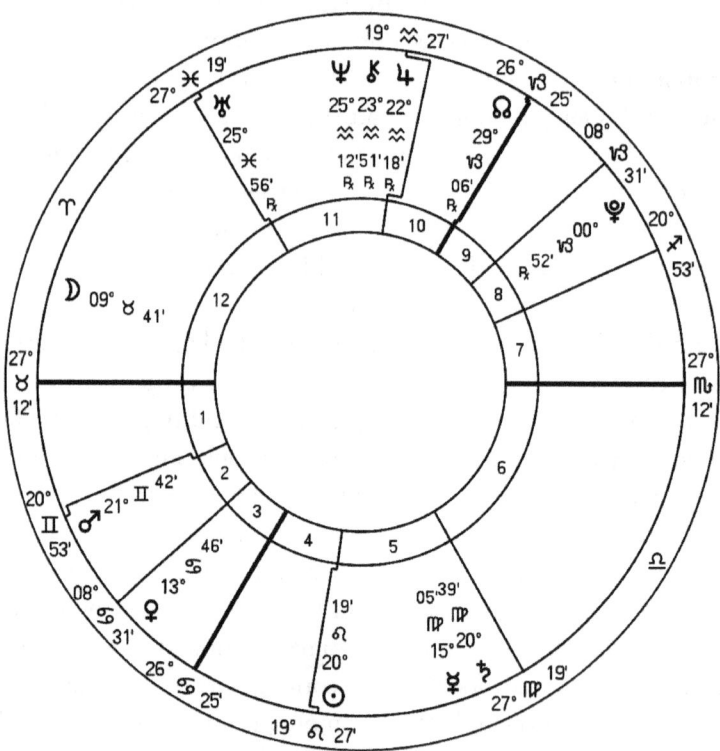

Carole: Data withheld for purposes of confidentiality

Audience (Carole): I've been here for ten years.

Clare: So that means we will cast the return for London. It's quite nice to go straight into this return chart knowing nothing about your natal chart. This will help us look for the main themes in the chart itself. What do you all see?

Audience: The Moon is unaspected.

Clare: That's right. And the only planet in fire is your Sun. And the only personal planet in water is Venus.

Audience: The Sun is in the fifth house which is great.

Clare: That's right, so looking at the houses, what do you think this chart is saying to Carole? What must she do this year, with the Sun in the fifth house?

Audience: She should be creative.

Clare: She must put herself first, mustn't she? This is a year for creative self expression, when Carole should do something she really wants to do. But we can see that the solar return chart is reflecting some major transits which are and have been opposing her natal Sun for quite a long time. Neptune, Chiron and Jupiter in Aquarius are all opposite that Sun. So we can say that there is a prolonged struggle for Carole between listening to her heart or her head. This is the classic Aquarius-Leo struggle, with the head working against the heart and vice versa. These oppositions are also across the fifth and eleventh houses, describing the tension between the individual and the group.

Imagine that Carole has come to you for a chart reading, you have looked at the solar return and you want to advise her what she should be doing next year, what might you want to say to her?

Audience: That she should be doing her own thing this year, and not get too involved in what everyone else thinks?

Clare: We know from the chart that Neptune and Chiron have been opposing Carole's natal Sun for several years. Both these planets, when aspecting the Sun, demand some kind of self sacrifice, and so we might imagine that she has had a few blows and may have lost some of her self confidence, clarity and focus. And now Jupiter has joined the Neptune-Chiron conjunction and will be making three transits over this conjunction, which makes these feelings even bigger. The classic interpretation of the Sun in the solar return fifth house is that this is a year for personal self expression and fulfilment, so perhaps this chart suggests that a rebalancing is necessary, that this is a year to regenerate, to put yourself first and to remember who you are. This can also be the year to take a gamble, to develop your gifts, so if there is anything you have been wanting to do, this solar return gives you permission to go for it.

Audience: With the stellium in the eleventh house, perhaps Carole is supposed to contribute to some group or other, in a Promethean way, because Neptune and Chiron have been dancing around opposite the Sun, so she may encounter situations where her dreams of belonging to a collective go sour and perhaps she gets disappointed? I have that trio squaring my Sun and that has been my experience.

Audience (Carole): I think it's right, because I am having this dilemma about whether to go back to Argentina or to stay here and that is all to do with relationships.

Clare: And of course the fifth house is also about love affairs.

Audience: Mars is sextile and trine that opposition, so it's ... that could be helpful, couldn't it, Mars in Gemini?

Clare: Or not, because Mars in Gemini might be saying: 'Shall I do this, shall I do that?', wanting to do both at the same time.

Audience: Yes but could it bring the two things together?

Clare: It can actually indicate a great deal of mental stress, I think, because Mars in Gemini might feel as if it is demanding a decision, but we have a difficult opposition here, which means you cannot easily go one way or the other.

Audience: It's a fixed opposition.

Clare: Yes, fixed and very tight, and Mars is giving it energy, which generates stress. And you may be feeling that in the body, since Mars is in the second house. So this is about finding some kind of way of accommodating both ends of this opposition. Do you see how helpful this could be in a consultation? You can identify the dilemma, knowing that both ends of this opposition need to be honoured, and Carole's task is to clarify what her head wants and what her heart wants. Of course this is a major configuration which doesn't just belong to the solar return chart but will show up in the general transits. It is not our job as astrologers to try and solve the problem, but just identifying and exploring the nature of the conflict can be enormously helpful in itself and should enable Carole to engage with the year ahead in a more conscious and creative way.

Audience: How do you think Carole could use that Mars constructively?

Clare: I would look for the ruler of that Mars, which is Mercury in a conjunction with Saturn, also in the fifth house and both in Virgo. This gives us clues about how Mars needs to function this year. Negatively, this might indicate a feeling of paralysis, of not being able to make a decision. Positively, we might suggest that Carole doesn't try and force herself to make a decision, but to be patient and take her time. Maybe, since this is in Virgo, we might encourage her to do something small and ritualistic, to write a journal for example, so that she can process her thoughts and give expression to her inner conflict, which will definitely help her digest what is going on.

Audience (Carole): Maybe I should just focus on my work this year, which is actually a good way of using that Mercury-Saturn in Virgo, because I work in a design studio, designing and making clothes in leather. It's an excellent place to learn because both the other designers in the studio are specialists and very experienced.

Audience: And with that Mercury-Saturn conjunction in the fifth house, isn't that about developing her own skills and talents?

Clare: Yes, and it is fascinating that you are working with leather, which is animal skin, and therefore ruled by Saturn. Developing your design and skills with leather is a wonderful description of the Saturn-Mercury in Virgo in the fifth house. And the square to Mars describes the cutting of the leather. So this could be an extremely creative year for you in terms of your work, and the solar return indicates that this is not just about working for the design studio, but that you need enough time and space this year to develop your own design skills and talents. The other point to notice is that the nodal axis is picking up the MC/IC axis of your solar return chart, with the north node on the Midheaven, which is to do with where you are going in life and where you are coming from. This indicates a significant change of direction this year, and it would be interesting to check when that node transits exactly onto the Midheaven, which will be around October this year.

Audience (Carole): That's interesting, because I am thinking about starting my own business this year, and so maybe I will know more about this in a few months' time. One of the reasons I want to do this is because it will give me more contact with where I come from, since I will be ordering my skins from Argentina. My problem at the moment is that I had a relationship with the owner of the studio a few years ago. He is extremely talented and creative, but he had a drink problem, so we broke it off, but it is awkward working with him because we are still very attracted to each other.

Clare: So starting your own business would be an excellent way of integrating both ends of this opposition, and finding room for both. And the relationship situation would be another explanation of the current, rather complex Neptune-Chiron-Jupiter oppositions to the Sun.

Audience: What about the unaspected Moon in the twelfth house? This is an excellent Moon, isn't it, because it is exalted in Taurus. But it is entirely alone.

Clare: There is a mutual reception between the Moon in Taurus and Venus in Cancer, so I would suggest that this year you should ensure that you have plenty of time to nurture yourself, and that contact with nature will be very important to you.

Audience: How about going on a retreat? Somewhere beautiful in the country? And also the twelfth house is the house of institutions of all sorts.

Audience (Carole): Well, that's one of the things I really feel I need at the moment.

Clare: That might be a very good idea. I have been thinking recently about how real creativity stems from the process of deliberate re-creation. It is not really about crashing forwards with the will all the time – it comes from somewhere else completely, and we need to create the time and space to allow that.

Lunar Returns

Lunar returns occur every 27.32 days, when the Moon returns exactly to its natal position, and so there are 13 lunar returns every year, sometimes 14. The focus of these return charts will be the house in which the Moon falls, which will be the area of our emotional concerns, emotional connections and describe the mood for the month in question. Astrologers usually cast a series of lunar returns to track the shifting emotions over a period of time. And this can help us navigate the lunar tides, indicating where we will be looking for emotional satisfaction and what nurtures us for that month, and of course this changes constantly. We can work creatively with these charts in that they can encourage us to go with the flow. So if the Moon is in the twelfth house for a month, then we can just retreat and spend some time by ourselves, if it is in the fifth house, then that is the month to go and play. And if it's in the eighth house, then we may need to connect deeply with our lover that month. Have any of you worked with your lunar returns?

Audience: I did in my analysis when I was just going once a month, although I was fairly new to astrology then. My analyst was working with astrology, but I didn't get anything much out of it. I think I find them difficult, because my Moon is in the twelfth house natally.

Clare: The lunar return charts seem to reflect our emotional condition that month, so they can give us permission to be more fluid and live more instinctively. Relevant questions to ask the lunar return chart are 'What will feed me this month? Where do I get my nurturing this month?' We know that the Moon is always needy, so there is really nothing to do except to nurture it. So try casting your own lunar return charts for a few months to see what you think about them. And remember that what we are feeling inside is not necessarily a reflection of what is going on in the world outside, and we all respond differently to different events.

Audience: So you would use the relocated chart for the lunar returns as well?

Clare: Yes, particularly because our feelings are so ephemeral, and very dependent on our environment, and we feel quite different in different places.

Mars Returns
Mars returns suggest the best way to assert our will, potency and individuality for the next two years. Imagine your natal Mars energy gradually being used up and running out of steam over a two year period, but every time it returns to its natal position it is plugged in again and our vitality and energy levels are recharged.

Audience: The fighting gear needs to be re-polished.

Clare: Yes, and so it is worth remembering that if someone comes for a reading just before their Mars return they may well be feeling exhausted. The Mars return chart, and the house in which Mars falls will show the quality and nature of the regeneration, and the new goals and directions for the following two years. Although this is the natal Mars, the specific themes will be different. So the questions would be: 'Where and how do we need to assert ourselves and take action? Where and how do we go about getting what we want?' As with all return charts, the angles will be important because they indicate how we are going to express that particular planetary energy out in the world. In the Mars return chart, the Ascendant indicates how we should be meeting challenges, and the Midheaven indicates our conscious goals for the period.

Audience: My Mars return is coming up in two months' time, and I have been having colds all the time recently, which I just can't shake off. So hopefully I will get some more energy at the Mars return.

Clare: Yes, I am sure that will happen. Now, with Mars, Jupiter, Saturn and even Chiron there can be three return charts, since they all have periods of retrogradation. So we need to check how many returns each of these planets has, and to take the last one as the official return chart, since it is that chart which sets the scene for the entire cycle to come.

Jupiter Returns

We usually have six or seven Jupiter cycles in our lifetime and, as we have already seen, each cycle has its own inherent meaning and describes a particular chapter of exploration and the growth of wisdom. The first cycle is just about exploring the world for the first time, the second cycle is about the development of our education, and in the third cycle we are exploring what it is like to be out in the real world as young adults, earning our own money and supporting ourselves. During the fourth cycle we are contributing real worth to the world, and the fifth cycle is normally about revisioning what is meaningful to us personally and going beyond our identification with the world, so that, during the sixth cycle we can find new meaning and fulfil a new vision which grows out of the second Saturn return.

As each Jupiter cycle comes to an end, the meaning it carried at the beginning has normally been outgrown and we start to feel bored and restless. As the return approaches, we find the enthusiasm and the faith to widen our horizons and embark on new adventures. And each of these cycles has its own birth chart, the Jupiter return, which indicates the themes and areas of focus for the next twelve years or so. It is definitely worth drawing up the chart of the start of the Jupiter cycle you are in at the moment, to see this for yourselves. Are you in the process of fulfilling Jupiter's plans for you? Have a look at the house which Jupiter falls in

– is this an area of expanding meaning and exploration for you at the moment?

Audience: So if you have a Neptune-Jupiter conjunction in your Jupiter return chart, does that mean you are stuck with Neptune for the next twelve years?

Clare: That's right, although of course that doesn't have to be negative. It just suggests that during this particular Jupiter cycle perhaps you should be living your dreams and fantasies, and perhaps art, or dance and music are going to hold particular meaning for you.

Chiron Returns

I don't have much experience working with Chiron return charts, but if the return itself symbolises resolution and self acceptance, then I would suggest that the Chiron return chart indicates how we can best use our gift to serve others, now that the personal cycle has been completed and, hopefully, resolved.

Saturn Returns

Most of us will have two Saturn returns and some of us will have three, and the Saturn return charts will tell us what we need to learn, to achieve and to make real during the next cycle. These charts describe the nature of the seed which is being planted and which will grow during the next twenty-nine years. So the questions to ask are: 'What does Saturn demand of me for the next 29 years? What do I need to learn now? Where is my work going to be?', because every return chart is interpreted in terms of the planet which is returning.

Audience (Gemma): I am about to have my Saturn return, and the return chart has Saturn exactly conjunct Venus on the Ascendant.

Clare: That is a very strong message about learning to value yourself by making a real personal commitment to the world. And it is about developing your personal skills and talents, because this conjunction is in Virgo, and that is about discrimination, isn't it? So what work do you actually do?

Audience (Gemma): I have been working in publishing for the last nine years, but I am doing a psychotherapy foundation course this year. I would like to change career eventually and work as a therapist, so I am trying to save up at the moment so that I can do the full training.

Clare: So your Saturn return chart has Virgo rising, with Saturn and Venus on that Ascendant. This means that you have the axis of service, Virgo/Pisces across your relationship axis, and you are already planning to develop the skills which will enable you to live this axis.

Audience (Gemma): But it is going to be very hard work.

Clare: Exactly, because we are talking about Saturn here. And of course, with the Venus-Saturn conjunction, you will value yourself according to your professional achievements. If we have clients who are coming up to their Saturn returns, then it is as if they have completed the previous curriculum, and it can be very helpful to have a look at the return chart itself to see what the syllabus is for the next cycle. In your particular case, it seems as if you are ready to build on the skills and experience you have gathered so far, and that you are quite clear about your new direction, and the new cycle of work and achievement which is about to begin. The first Saturn return chart normally indicates how and where we can best contribute to the world and achieve professional recognition and status. The middle Saturn cycle is often extremely effective in this way. We would read the second Saturn return chart slightly differently. When we are approaching the age of 59, it is time to let go of the previous cycle, since professional status and recognition in the eyes of the world is no longer relevant or appropriate. Rather, Saturn requires us to fully and actively re-engage with the world, but this is usually about making a more personal connection, often to nature. And then the sixth cycle of Jupiter comes along and gives us the faith and enthusiasm to do just that.

LESSON 7

Lunations, the Nodal Cycle and Eclipses

As we already know from our study of cycles, new Moons signify new beginnings and full Moons signify culmination and completion. The monthly lunar cycles are going on in the background all the time, gradually working their way around the chart each year, and occasionally falling on a planet or angle in the natal chart. Here is a table showing the new Moons and full Moons during 2009.

Date	Time: GMT	New Moon	Full Moon
11 January	3:27 am		21°♋02'
26 January	7:56 am	6°♒30'	
9 February	2:50 pm		20°♌60'
25 February	1:35 am	6°♓35'	
11 March	2:39 am		20°♍40''
26 March	4:07 pm	6°♈08'	
9 April	2:56 pm		19°♎53'
25 April	3:24 am	5°♉04'	
9 May	4:02 am		18°♏41'
24 May	12:12 pm	3♊28'	
7 June	6:13 pm		17°♐07'
22 June	7:36 pm	1°♋30'	
7 July	9:22 am		15°♑24'
22 July	2:36 am	29°♋27'	
6 Aug	00:55 am		13°♒43'
20 Aug	10:02 am	27°♌32'	
4 Sept	4:04 pm		12°♓15'
18 Sept	6:44 pm	25°♍59'	
4 Oct	6:11 am		11°♈10'
18 Oct	5:34 am	24°♎59'	
2 Nov	7:14 pm		10°♉30'

16 Nov	7:15 pm	24° ♏ 34'	
2 Dec	7:31 am		10° ♊ 15'
16 Dec	12:02 pm	24° ♐ 40'	
31 Dec	7:14 pm		10° ♋ 15'

So the new and full Moons set up a rhythmic or tidal ebb and flow of repeated beginnings and endings, breathing in and breathing out, drawing in and letting go. This is an interesting rhythm to follow since, as you can see, the full Moons generally occur in the opposite signs and houses from the new Moons. The energetic focus of new activity will be where the new Moons occur in the chart, suggesting where we might be putting our energy for that month, and the full Moons on the other side of our charts suggest where we might be letting go. If we are actively following the Moon's cycles, then we can use this ebb and flow of lunar energy to support us as we ride the emotional tides of change.

Occasionally, a new or full Moon will fall on a natal planet or angle, so it will be of particular personal significance. That natal planet or angle will be emphasised and emotionally charged for a very short period of time, usually for one day, on the actual date of the lunation.

A new Moon on the Descendant, for example, might indicate a new relationship, or the beginning of a new chapter in an existing relationship. Conversely, a full Moon on the Descendant could indicate the emotional realisation that a relationship has ended.

A full Moon on the MC will point to the culmination, result or outcome of an existing phase. This might indicate the date on which the results of a previous job application or interview are made known, or the completion of a project at work, or recognition for work done. Or it might coincide with the decision to look for another job, or even perhaps being made redundant. The planet or angle receiving the lunation will be emotionally charged.

Audience: How close does the lunation have to be to something in the natal chart for it to have an effect?

Clare: Well, the closer the better. I would suggest a maximum orb of 1° 30'. Now, the interesting thing about these lunations is that every 19 years, the phases of the Moon recur on the same days of the same months, normally within about two hours. This is known as the *Metonic Period*, named after the Greek astronomer Meton, who lived in the fifth century BC. The astrological significance of the Metonic Period is that every 19 years the meaning of the previous lunation will *resonate* powerfully once again for the individual. Memories of events and feelings which occurred 19 years previously will return, so whenever a lunation occurs on a natal planet or angle, we should always give some thought to what was going on 19 years previously, since old memories are likely to surface and this is an opportunity to complete any emotional processing which may be left over from the last lunation. Our emotions have their own timing, and old feelings can remain buried in the body and psyche for a very long time. So, used consciously, these repeating 19-year lunation cycles present us with an opportunity to revisit old memories and release any emotional residues.

Audience: This is interesting because I have noticed from the table that there is a full Moon on 4th September on my Sun in Pisces in the fifth house. I have been feeling very sad because my daughter, who was actually born 19 years ago, is leaving home to go to university at the end of September. So I have been thinking a great deal about the last 19 years and feeling the loss very keenly.

Clare: That's an excellent example, and time for you to take time to acknowledge your feelings and to let her go, although of course that is very sad. However, the new Moons in Leo, Virgo and Libra around this time indicate that this is a good time to think about your own plans (Leo) now that you will have more time to yourself (Virgo) and perhaps to gain strength and support from your partner (Libra)?

Nodal Cycle

The nodal cycle is slightly shorter than the Metonic Period. The nodal axis is, in a way, completely separate from the rest of the chart, it is a doorway or magical threshold between this and other worlds, moving one degree retrograde every 18.6 days, spending 19 months in a sign, and its entire cycle around the chart is 18.6 years. The pattern for half nodal returns, when the transiting nodal axis is the reverse of our natal nodal axis, and full nodal returns is as follows:

Half Nodal Returns Age	Nodal Returns Age
9.25	18.6
27.75	37
46.5	55.75
65	74.5

This cycle of the nodal axis is important for two reasons. Firstly, as we saw last term, the axis gradually moves backwards, in the opposite direction from all the other planets. The nodal axis is an axis of integration, working in the background as we review, process and digest, assimilating and releasing our life experience. So as we follow the transiting nodal axis around our chart we need to ask ourselves: 'What has to be remembered' 'What has to be integrated'?

Secondly, it is on or near the nodal axis that eclipses occur. As we saw last term, it is on this axis that the Sun, Moon and Earth come into alignment, and this is therefore the symbolic meeting point of spirit, soul and body, the axis of destiny, the threshold between this and other worlds. The transiting nodal axis tends to personify, and it is here that we meet significant people who seem to recognise or nurture our potential. The houses through which the nodal axis is transiting will indicate the areas of life in which significant encounters occur. Both ends of the axis are involved, although it is on the transiting south node that we tend to meet people from the past, and on the transiting north node that we tend to meet liminal figures who may be in our lives for just a short time but who help us move on.

The nodal squares and half returns, when the transiting axis squares or opposes our natal axis, represent turning points and opportunities for personal integration, since this is the axis where opposites meet, and we can build on, or process and release, past experiences.

The nodal return is a time of new beginnings and we can feel a surge of energy which feeds our imagination and opens up new possibilities. Loss and separation is a necessary part of clearing the way for the future, but the appearance of helpers, guides and mentors helps us move forwards. The urge to follow our destiny is strong at this time.

Audience: Can you say more about these significant people who come into our lives, Clare?

Clare: Well, first of all, the houses across which our natal nodal axis falls describe the people who will be particularly significant to us for the whole of our lives. So for example, with the nodal axis across the fifth/eleventh house axis, then it is our children, friends and colleagues who will change our lives, be the agents of our destiny, if you like. With the nodal axis across the third/ninth house axis, then it will be our siblings, neighbours and teachers, or people from other cultures who will be of particular significance. This will be a lifelong pattern. As far as the transiting nodal axis is concerned, then our most creative approach is to keep our eyes and ears open for significant encounters in the areas of life described by the houses through which the nodal axis is transiting. This is where it often feels as if we are being given a kick, which, although it may not be welcome at first, brings about a significant change of direction and puts us on a more authentic and meaningful path.

So, when the nodal axis is transiting through our first and seventh houses, there may well be a crisis and a turning point in our relationship, and this will be driven by our partner (seventh house), but represent a new beginning for us personally (first house). If the north node is transiting the seventh house, then someone significant is likely to come into our lives, and if the south node is transiting the seventh house, then it might be time for someone who has been significant to pass out of our lives.

Audience: How interesting – I got divorced when the south node was transiting through my seventh house, and I have nothing to do with my ex-husband now.

Clare: The same applies to all the other house axes. With the nodal axis transiting through the second and eighth houses we should be looking out for encounters with people who affect our physical and emotional resources. This may be someone who really values and supports us, or a family member from whom we inherit money. With the nodal axis transiting through the third and ninth houses, then our teachers, students or siblings will be the omen speakers. A philosophy or religion, or a particular book we might read at that time may alter the way we see ourselves and our lives. With the nodal axis transiting through the fourth and tenth houses, our parents or family or authority figures might help us to change direction, and in the fifth and eleventh houses some important guidance and wisdom might come to us through our children, lovers, friends or colleagues, or even through groups. Finally, with the nodal axis transiting through the sixth and twelfth houses, we should be looking for clues from our work colleagues, animal guides, ghosts, spirits and dreams. I would like to read you a passage on the mediation of angels from Thomas Moore's *Re-Enchantment of Everyday Life*:

> "If we are seriously interested in knowing the deep roots and essential characteristics of our own nature and fate, then we might do well to keep our eyes and ears open for angels, who perform the hermetic function of guiding the soul. In our communities and friendships, if we were to look for the deeply hidden presence of the angel in others, we might get past all the personal, psychological judgments that keep love out of our lives."[1]

Looking again at the table of lunations for 2009, I have added the positions of the nodes:

Date	Time GMT	New Moon	Full Moon	Mean Nodal Axis	Eclipses
11 January	3:27 am		21°♋02'	10°♒24'	
26 January	7:56 am	6°♓30'		9°♒37'	Solar Eclipse
9 February	2:50 pm		21°♌00'	8°♒52'	
25 February	1:35 am	6°♈35'		8°♒1'	
11 March	2:39 am		20°♍40'	7°♒17'	
26 March	4:07 pm	6°♉08'		6°♒29'	
9 April	2:56 pm		19°♎53'	5°♒45'	
25 April	3:24 am	5°♊04'		4°♒54'	
9 May	4:02 am		18°♏41'	4°♒09'	
24 May	12:12 pm	3°♋28'		3°♒22'	
7 June	6:13 pm		17°♐07'	2°♒37'	
22 June	7:36 pm	1°♌30'		1°♒49'	

Date	Time				
7 July	9:22 am		15°♑24'	1°♒02'	
22 July	2:36 am	29°♍27'		0°♒14'	Solar Eclipse
6 Aug	00:55 am		13°♒43'	29°♑26'	
20 Aug	10:02 am	27°♎32'		28°♑42'	
4 Sept	4:04 pm		12°♓15'	27°♑54'	
18 Sept	6:44 pm	25°♏59'		27°♑10'	
4 Oct	6:11 am		11°♈10'	26°♑19'	
18 Oct	5:34 am	24°♐59'		25°♑35'	
2 Nov	7:14 pm		10°♉30'	24°♑47'	
16 Nov	7:15 pm	24°♏34'		24°♑02'	
2 Dec	7:31 am		10°♊15'	23°♑12'	
16 Dec	12:02 pm	24°♐40'		22°♑27'	
31 Dec	7:14 pm		10°♋15'	21°♑39'	Lunar Eclipse

You will see from this table how the nodal axis shifts in July from Aquarius/Leo to Capricorn/Cancer, and so that is where the solar and lunar eclipses will occur, every six months when the Sun is in these signs.

Audience: How can you work out if it is going to be a solar or a lunar eclipse?

Clare: A solar eclipse occurs at the new Moon when the Moon and Sun are in conjunction from the point of view of the Earth. A lunar eclipse occurs at the full Moon when the Moon and Sun are in opposition from the point of view of the Earth. Whether they will be solar or lunar eclipses depends on the Moon's relationship to the Sun at the time, and this varies from year to year.

ECLIPSES

Eclipses are of considerable importance when it comes to timing events, and they have always been associated with the workings of fate. You will find the Moon's phases and the dates of the solar and lunar eclipses at the bottom right hand side of each page of the American Ephemerides for the 20th and 21st century. Solar and lunar eclipses occur at new and full

Moons respectively, but only when these coincide with one of the nodes and only when the Sun, Earth and Moon are more or less on the same plane. If the ecliptic, or plane of the Sun, exactly coincided with the plane of the Moon's orbit, there would be a solar eclipse every new Moon and a lunar eclipse at every full Moon. But the Moon's orbit is inclined at an angle of approximately 5° to the ecliptic, so eclipses can only occur approximately every six months, when a new or full  Moon occurs near one of the nodes. Total and annular eclipses occur within 9° of the nodal axis, whereas partial[2] and appulse[3] eclipses can occur up to a distance of 19° of the nodal axis.

Solar Eclipses
It is interesting that, although the diameter of the Sun is 400 times greater than that of the Moon, they are roughly the same size when viewed from the Earth, so the Moon can block out the Sun's light when it passes in front of the Sun. Solar eclipses can only occur at a new Moon, when the Sun and Moon are in conjunction. They can be total, partial or annular.

The distance of the Moon from the Earth varies by about 10%. A total solar eclipse occurs when the Moon is at perigee, at its closest point to the Earth, when it can completely cover the disk of the Sun. The cone of shadow (umbra) produces an area on the Earth's surface, never

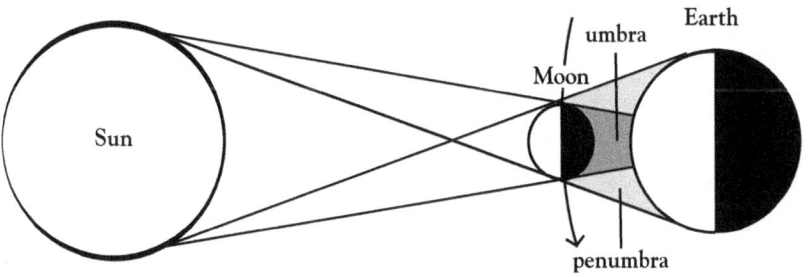

Solar eclipse

more than 170 miles wide, where the total eclipse is visible, around which is an area of semi-shadow (penumbra), visible for several thousands of miles either side of the totality, which is where a partial solar eclipse is visible.

An annular eclipse occurs when the Moon is at apogee, at its furthest distance from the Earth and does not completely cover the disc of the Sun but leaves a solar ring around it.

Annular Eclipse

Lunar eclipses can only occur at a full Moon, when the Sun and Moon are in opposition and when the Moon passes into the Earth's shadow. When they occur, lunar eclipses are visible over the whole night hemisphere of the Earth and can last for up to two hours, since the Earth's full shadow, the umbra, is greater than the diameter of the Moon. If only part of the Moon passes into the Earth's umbra, there is a partial lunar eclipse, whilst if it passes only through the penumbra and misses the umbra altogether, it is a penumbral eclipse.

Audience: But why don't lunar eclipses happen every month when the Sun and Moon are in opposition?

Clare: It depends on the alignment of the Sun and Moon. The plane of the Moon's orbit is not the same as the plane of the Sun's orbit, so the Moon can be up to 5° above or below the ecliptic. So if the Moon is high, for example, then it won't pass into the Earth's shadow, and we will see its entire face at the full Moon.

Audience: So the Moon is always at 0° latitude for all eclipses, and that also explains why there can be a Sun-Moon conjunction without a solar eclipse occurring?

Clare: Exactly. Moving on smartly from all this technical information, eclipses are like super-lunations, heralding a significant change of direction.

Audience: But are eclipses always negative?

Clare: I don't think so. Traditionally they are supposed to have a negative effect, because the eclipses are where the great celestial dragon was thought to swallow up either the Sun or Moon.

Eclipses will eventually pick up angles or planets in your birth chart, and when that happens it will be extremely significant, with that angle or planet being highlighted and strongly emphasised for up to 18 months before and after the eclipse. And of course we are not always ready to make significant changes in our lives, even though this is indicated by the eclipses. But we can certainly use eclipses actively and creatively to help us work with the changes they indicate, the nature of which depends on the particular planet or angle they are focusing on. So we can work with, rather than against, them.

Audience: This year I have a lunar eclipse falling across my Ascendant/Descendant axis.

Clare: So this will emphasise the relationship between yourself and others, and will indicate some kind of significant completion or culmination.

It is worth pointing out at this stage that, just like the Metonic Period and the Nodal cycle, there is also a repeating eclipse cycle known as the Saros cycle. And this too is significant in forecasting work. At some point during the second millennium BC, the Babylonians discovered that the same type of eclipse – solar, lunar, annular or partial – occurs every 18 years, 11 and one-third days, but not necessarily in the same place. This is the length of the Saros, or repeating eclipse cycle. And every 71 Saros cycles, the eclipses will return to the same degree.

Notes
1. Thomas Moore, *The Re-Enchantment of Everyday Life*, p.345
2. An annular eclipse occurs when the Moon covers the centre of the Sun, but not its edges, leaving a ring of the Sun visible around its edges.
3. An appulse lunar eclipse is a penumbral eclipse where the Moon enters only the penumbra of the Earth.

LESSON 8

Transits: Case Study of Dante Gabriel Rossetti

One of the best ways to learn about transits is to work with actual examples, and I always think that one of the main qualities we need as astrologers is a fascination with other people's lives and an interest in reading biographies. It is truly astonishing to see how the various forecasting techniques manifest throughout an individual's life, whether or not they have any knowledge of astrology.

So I am going to use the chart of the pre-Raphaelite artist Dante Gabriel Rossetti, who lived an eventful life at an extremely interesting time in history. We will study his chart as I tell you his story, and see how some of the major transits worked out in his life. We will then use his chart to look at the progressions and directions, so that you can see how the forecasting layers gradually build up.

Dante Gabriel Rossetti was born on 12th May 1828 in London at 4.30 am LMT and has Taurus rising at 25°43'.

There are three major themes in this chart. The first is the strong Taurean emphasis, with Chiron, Moon, Mercury and Sun in Taurus, as well as the Ascendant. Taurus is a gentle and sensuous sign, ruled by Venus and the seat of the Moon's exaltation. So it is well attuned to the feminine; and indeed Venus, which rules all these Taurus placements, is itself in Cancer in the second house, which is itself ruled by the Moon. So there is a mutual reception between the Moon in Taurus and Venus in Cancer. With three personal planets and Chiron in the twelfth house, we know that Rossetti needed solitude, contact with nature and an environment which was beautiful and peaceful, and which supported the enjoyment of the simple, tangible pleasures of life. He needed to work with his hands and with material substance and had a real feeling for the earth and for the feminine. Taurus is a gentle, peace loving sign, and extremely persistent. Male Taureans are normally sensuous and charming. With Mercury in Taurus he would take time to make up his mind but, once decided, would stick to his ground. The earth signs have strong foundations, rooted in history and tradition.

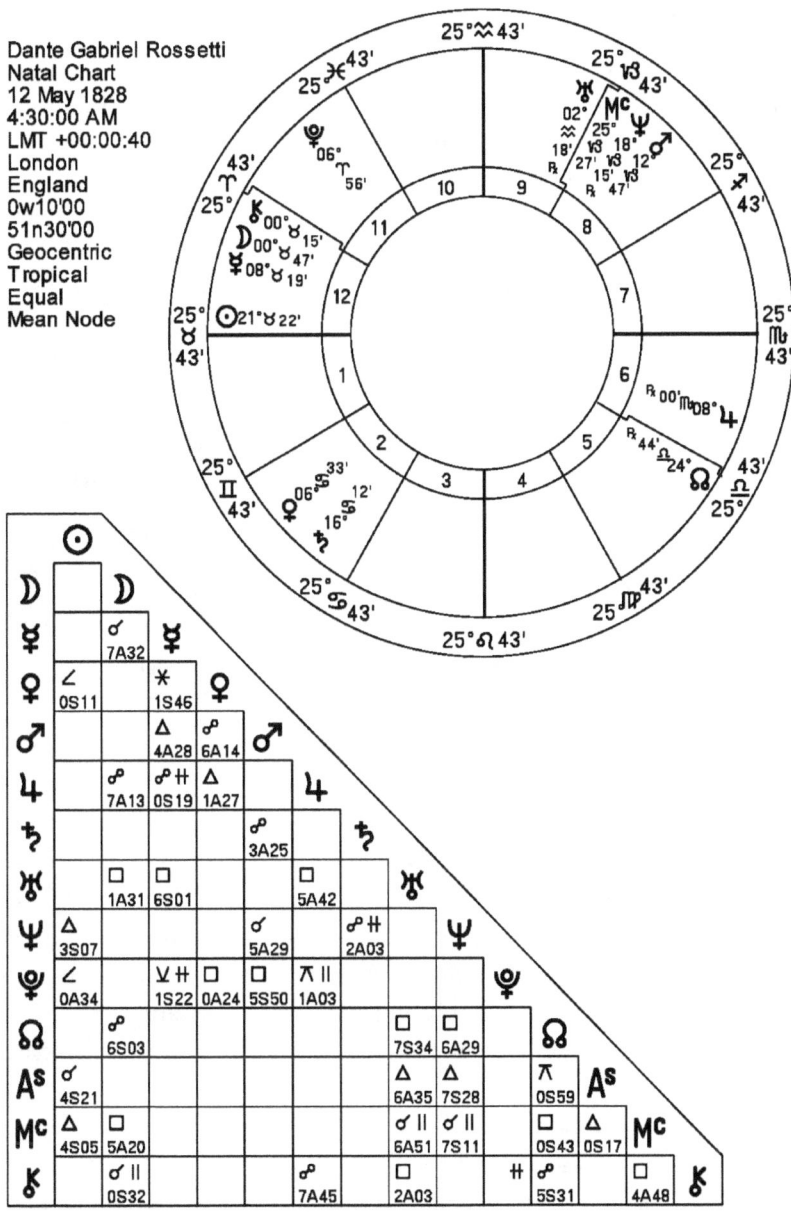

With Chiron in a tight conjunction to the Moon, however, we know that Rossetti would have felt estranged and alienated from the safety and comfort which is normally necessary for a Taurean Moon, and so we would imagine that he would try to 'fix' these feelings of insecurity by becoming extremely materialistic and possessive. Eventually, he would need to learn to trust his own instincts, no matter how unacceptable they may have been to others.

Pluto is in an almost exact square to Venus, adding a powerful charge of intensity and passion to his values.

The next major theme in Rossetti's chart is the powerful T-square formed by the opposition of retrograde Jupiter in Scorpio in the sixth house to the three twelfth house Taurus planets Chiron, Moon and Mercury, with the radical and highly charged, high-voltage Uranus in Aquarius at the apex.

Dante Gabriel Rossetti
Self Portrait – Aged 19

Examining this T-square, the twelfth house story deepens. Rossetti's father was Italian, a celebrated and controversial Dante scholar and political exile, and Professor of Italian at Kings College in London. Rossetti had three siblings, all of whom were remarkable, the most famous being the poet Christina Rossetti. This was a particularly gifted, creative and unconventional family, as indicated by Aquarius on the tenth house cusp and Leo on the fourth house cusp.

The twelfth house planets in Taurus provide a particularly accurate picture of a displaced family in exile (Moon-Chiron) – father (Sun), mother (Moon) and siblings (Mercury). With Jupiter retrograde in Scorpio in the sixth house and Uranus in Aquarius in the ninth house, this T-square describes Rossetti's family and ancestral inheritance. He clearly comes from a long line of radical, independent and somewhat subversive free thinkers.

The life and work of the 13th century political exile and poet Alghieri Dante, was a lifelong source of inspiration for Rossetti and, as we would expect, there is strong synastry between the two charts.[1] Rossetti's Midheaven-Neptune conjunction picks up Dante's nodal axis, his tenth house cusp is on Dante's Moon and his Chiron, Moon, Mercury stellium is on Dante's Uranus. So this is an example of the way that birth charts continue to resonate through time, in this case for over 500 years. Both men had their Suns in the twelfth house and both found artistic inspiration through the ideal of the feminine, in the form of a muse. In Dante's case it was Beatrice, a woman whom he saw from a distance only once or twice in his life but who inspired his writing and even appears as a guide in his great work *The Divine Comedy*. For Rossetti, it was a series of artistic models, notably Elizabeth Siddal and Jane Morris, as we shall see. So this also takes us back to the importance of the women in Rossetti's chart and life.

The third major theme in Rossetti's chart is the Mars-Neptune conjunction on the Midheaven, all in Capricorn, suggesting artistic drive and ambition. And there is an interesting set of oppositions here too, with Saturn opposite Neptune and Venus opposite Mars. With both Venus and Saturn in nostalgic Cancer, Rossetti longed for an idealised past and for the idealised muse – both of which he clearly expressed in his painting and writing. Since both Venus and Saturn are ruled by the Moon, tightly conjunct Chiron in the twelfth house, he often portrayed tragic and painful themes, fuelled by his deep sense of alienation from history, family and nature.

In his late teens, Rossetti studied at the Royal Academy of Art in London, but rebelled against the artistic conventions of the day, which is not surprising when we know his chart. He thought the art of his day was static and dull, agreeing with John Ruskin's comment that it was limited to "cattle pieces and sea pieces and fruit pieces and family pieces – the eternal brown cows in ditches, white sails in squalls, and sliced lemons in saucers and foolish faces in simpers". He wanted to do something more radical and different, so in 1848 he left the Royal Academy at the age of 20 and started studying under an independent teacher.

This was the year of Rossetti's Chiron opposition, a strongly vocational aspect, with Chiron transiting his sixth house and constellating his entire fixed T-Square, not least the square to Uranus and opposition to the Moon and Mercury. He realised that he could not, or would not conform to the accepted artistic standards of his time. He was a rebel, a maverick and an outsider.

This was also the year when transiting Uranus squared his Midheaven, and since Rossetti's nodal axis is exactly square to his Midheaven, the Uranus transit triggered a radical and uncompromising change of direction in his life and career. He decided to start a new artistic move-

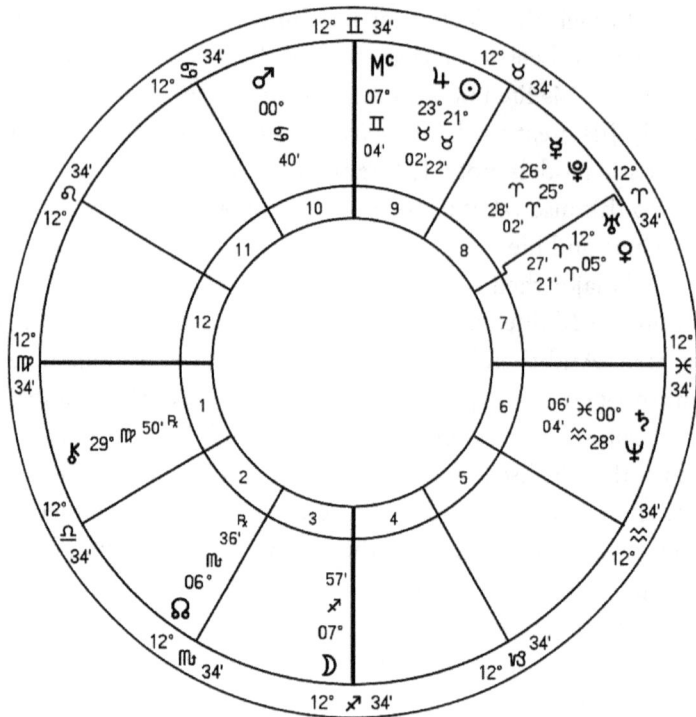

Rossetti – Solar Return for 1846

ment dedicated to the revival of beauty, magic, passion, myth and symbolism in art, and gathered a group of people around him, which he called the Pre-Raphaelite Brotherhood or PRB.

Here is the solar return for 1846, when Rossetti was 18 and the year he went to the Royal Academy. As you can see, this is a fiery chart, with Mercury and Venus in Aries and the Moon in Sagittarius. Imagine that he has come to you for a reading, wanting to know how he should be maximising his creative potential, and if he was doing the right thing. We can see that Mercury (school) is sextile Neptune (art), and the Sun is conjunct Jupiter in the ninth house, so he should definitely be developing his talents and expanding his horizons in a meaningful way this year. And Jupiter is very comfortable in the ninth house. Both angles are ruled by Mercury, the planet of learning, and the Moon in Sagittarius is angular, on the IC, supporting the Sun-Jupiter conjunction. So we know that this is an exciting year to be a student, and, with the

Moon in Sagittarius on the IC, to be studying in this august place with the most eminent teachers of his day. So it seems as if he would feel at home here, and invest tremendous enthusiasm and energy into this new venture. Now, imagine that someone with this solar return chart had come to you for a consultation, wanting to know if they should accept an administrative job they had been offered or take the year off and walk to the base camp on Everest, then I think it is clear from the chart which of those options they should take, and this is the value of the solar return. It will be 19 years before the Moon returns to this same position, so it is important to make the most of it.

But we can also see what is going to happen. The Sun's ruler in a solar return chart is always important, and in this case both Jupiter and the Sun are ruled by Venus, which is in Aries and conjunct Uranus. What does that indicate?

Audience: Pioneering. And rebellion against the other, since they are in the seventh house?

Clare: Yes, this combination in Aries is fairly radical, and about doing what you want to do and doing it now. There are two major indicators of the rebellion to come, one to do with Venus, the Sun ruler, and the other to do with Mercury, the solar return chart ruler and ruler of both angles. Mercury is conjunct Pluto, also in Aries, in the eighth house of crisis. So how is he going to express himself that year? Perhaps this indicates a radical change in his thinking? Perhaps he feels that his ideas are sabotaged? Or perhaps he will become the saboteur? In fact, this had a positive effect, because out of this crisis of ideas the pre-Raphaelite movement was born, which had enormous collective influence.

Audience: I have just noticed that the Sun-Jupiter conjunction is unaspected.

Clare: Yes, which means that it is powerfully charged, obsessive and autonomous. An unaspected Sun in a solar return makes it burn very bright because it is not being moderated or translated or integrated with any other planetary principles. In this case, Jupiter is in the same condition, which magnifies its brightness and makes it even more compulsive, I would imagine. Let's see how this solar return chart compares to the natal chart.

Audience: The Venus-Uranus conjunction is on his Pluto in the eleventh, so perhaps he can't bear groups unless they are his group.

Clare: Good, and the unaspected Jupiter-Sun conjunction is sitting right on his natal Ascendant, giving it prominence. You can also see that the nodal axis is transiting natal Jupiter, indicating a change of direction in his work and technique. Jupiter describes what we live for in a deeper sense, the god which we serve. So whenever the nodal axis is in aspect to Jupiter it indicates a profound shift in our beliefs. So I hope you can see for yourselves how valuable these solar return charts are.

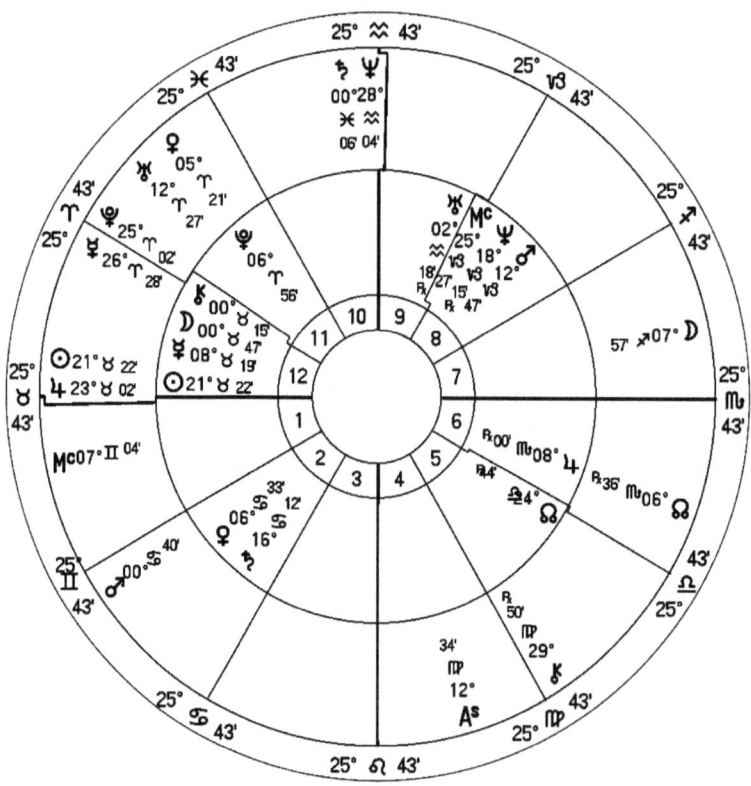

Rossetti – Natal Chart (inner) and Solar Return (outer) for 1846

Now, in 1850, at the age of 20, Rossetti met Elizabeth Siddal. The third of seven children, Elizabeth's father ran an ironmongery business in Southwark. Like her sisters, she became a dressmaker and milliner and was living with her large family above her father's shop off the Old Kent Road when Rossetti first met her. He and his friends persuaded her to become their model and before long he was claiming that he had found in her 'the image of his soul' and in her famous hair 'the golden veil through

Elizabeth Siddal
An early portrait by Dante

which he beheld his dreams'. Rossetti had met his muse, the woman who would inspire his work in both painting and writing for the rest of his life.

The transits paint a very clear picture of the immense significance to Rossetti of this meeting. There is a radical transiting conjunction of Pluto and Uranus right at the beginning of Taurus, and Rossetti is now under the powerful influence of his Uranus square Uranus, with transiting Uranus and Pluto conjunct his natal Moon-Chiron conjunction. Transiting Neptune, which carries our ideals and dreams, is exactly trine his natal Venus in Cancer. So we can understand what a powerful stimulant this encounter was. What other important transit is occurring around the age of 20?

Audience: The waning square in the Saturn cycle?

Clare: Exactly, and this of course represents a significant threshold and something of a rite of passage, as do all the hard aspects in the Saturn cycle. Rossetti is growing up, and with natal Saturn in Cancer we can see that he is in the process of transferring his emotional allegiance from his family to Elizabeth. Soon afterwards, they became unofficially engaged, and remained so for 14 years. She was not officially introduced to Rossetti's family until after his father's death because, being socially inferior, she would not have been acceptable to him.

Ophelia
John Everett Millais

One of the most famous paintings of Elizabeth is as Ophelia, painted by John Everett Millais. The story goes that she had to lie in a bath for hours while this was being painted, which caused a serious bout of pneumonia. This painting of Ophelia, a woman so badly treated by Hamlet that she drowned herself, turned out to be somewhat prophetic. It is one of many images of the suffering feminine which became such a hallmark of the PRB's paintings, and an apt expression of Rossetti's Chiron-Moon conjunction in Taurus. In fact, Lizzie was an extremely good artist in her own right, and was given a scholarship to enable her to cease being a model and develop her own talent.

Audience: Can we see the solar return chart for this year?

Clare: Yes. Now you will remember the importance of a new Moon in the solar return chart, and here we have the Sun and Moon in the same house and in the same sign, both angular as they straddle the Midheaven, with the Moon just separating from the conjunction. The new Moon is, literally, a *conjunctio*, symbolising balance, wholeness and harmony between Sun and Moon, male and female. And in Taurus this is a very sensuous combination, with Jupiter rising in earth too.

The other main thing which immediately stands out in this chart is the powerful mutable grand cross, with the Venus-Chiron opposition

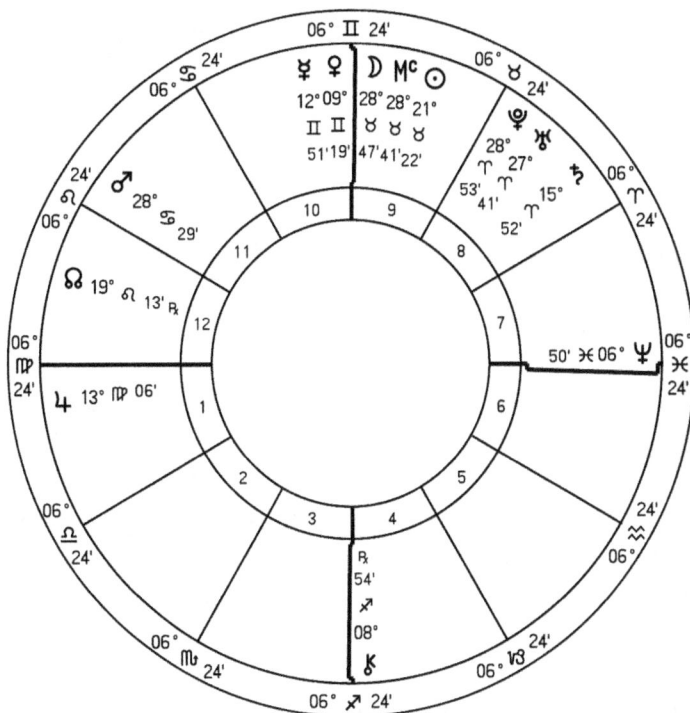

Rossetti – Solar Return for 1850

square to the Jupiter-Neptune opposition. And Neptune is angular, right on the Descendant. Can you have a go at interpreting this?

Audience: Idealisation in relationships? And a longing to be healed by the other?

Audience: And disappointment or deception, because of Neptune squaring the Chiron-Venus opposition.

Clare: Yes, and with Neptune in Pisces exactly on the Descendant, the boundaries between you and the other are totally non-existent. So it's about falling into a dream or a fantasy of the other and through the other, isn't it? And this is a dream which carries enormous meaning, although the pain of it is buried in the fourth house.

Audience: And I also want to say disappointment in terms of unrealistic expectations of the other to be the redeemer?

Audience: So you are looking for a saviour to come into your life. Someone to rescue you.

Clare: Exactly. And what kind of saviour, with Neptune square Venus?

Audience: A muse!

Audience: Mercury is also there, conjunct to Venus. Would you bring that in too?

Clare: Yes, definitely. If you remember, Mercury and Venus are always very important in a solar return chart because they serve the Sun. So this is clearly an immensely significant year. We have the angular Sun-Moon conjunction, with Jupiter in Virgo in the first house bringing meaning – the perfect ideal of the feminine. Both Neptune and Jupiter are the planets of god, and they connect with the Venus-Chiron opposition. So it's the vulnerable, impossible, divine woman who knocked him for six this year.

Clearly, this is a particularly strong solar return chart. Some of them are and some of them are not, but when you get close angular planets and a tight grand cross like this, then you know you are really onto something. And in fact you can see that the Moon is only 5' from the Midheaven.

So, how does this fit in with the natal chart? The MC/IC of the solar return chart is picking up the natal Ascendant/Descendant, so his professional focus for the year involves relationships.

And the Midheaven, Moon, Venus and Mercury are right there in the natal first house, so the emphasis is on Rossetti himself, on his needs, values and ideas.

Audience: And Chiron is in the seventh house.

Clare: Yes, which is rather chilling in relation to what eventually happened to this relationship, which, at the end of the day, was all

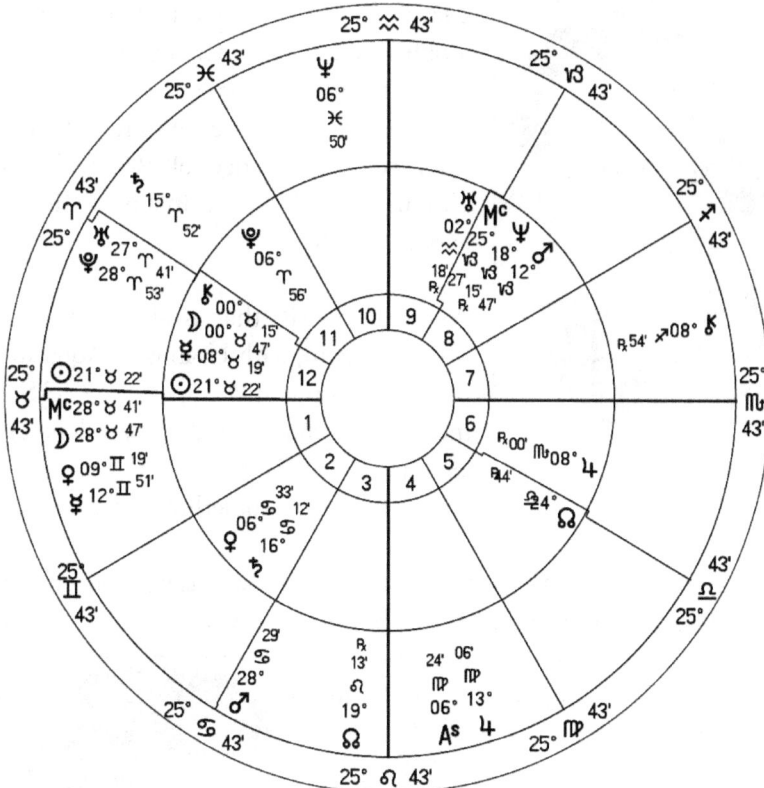

Rossetti – Natal Chart (inner) and Solar Return (outer) for 1850

about him, and very little about Lizzie herself. These are the years when Pluto is transiting Rossetti's tight Moon-Chiron conjunction. And this is interesting because, if you have ever studied Ted Hughes' chart, he also had a tight Moon-Chiron conjunction, and two wives who committed suicide. And here is another man with an exact Moon-Chiron conjunction, and Lizzie also committed suicide.

Moving on to Rossetti's Saturn return, what do you think the themes are likely to be?

Audience: This would be a time when he will take stock of everything he has achieved so far, and will be ready to move forwards and develop from there. With natal Saturn in Cancer in the second house the themes are likely to be about his values, about the past and the feminine. And perhaps family again?

Self Portrait – aged 27
Dante Gabriel Rossetti

Clare: That's right, that's what we will be looking for. The other significant transit occurring at the same time was Uranus transiting over the natal Ascendant. Again, from your knowledge of Rossetti's natal Uranus, how do you think he is likely to experience this?

Audience: Well, that is about the whole T-square again, with Uranus in Aquarius in the ninth house at the apex, isn't it? Some more radical change, and a new independent approach – a personal breakthrough, the opportunity to do something different.

Clare: Exactly. In 1857, when Rossetti was 29 he was introduced to the artists William Morris and Edward Burne-Jones, who had met at Oxford University and they secured a commission to paint the ceiling of the Debating Hall in the Oxford Union building. They decided to paint a large scheme of Arthurian murals, depicting the mythic story of Lancelot and Guinevere, and in fact you can still see this mural, although it is very faded now. This is the year he met two other women who would become significant models in the PRB, Fanny Cornforth and Jane Burden, who was spotted by Rossetti and Burne-Jones at a theatre in Oxford.

Jane Burden
Dante Gabriel Rossetti

Jane Burden was to play an important role in Rossetti's life. Both he and William Morris became obsessed by her, and the following year he broke off his engagement to Lizzie Siddal. You can see from this early drawing the strong features and the hair which are such a hallmark of the PRB's models.

A famous early painting of Jane by William Morris depicts her as the mythic figure of Isolde, the Irish princess betrothed to King Mark of

Cornwall. In the myth, Tristan was sent to Ireland to bring Isolde back to be married to King Mark, but he fell in love with her, so the story is about rivalry, and two men in love with the same woman.

Audience: And she chose William Morris?

Clare: Yes, that's right. And I am sure you can imagine how painful this was for Rossetti, with his Saturn in Cancer, Moon-Chiron conjunction in Taurus and Venus-Pluto square. Two years later, in 1859, William Morris and Jane Burden were married.

Audience: So he went back and married Lizzie?

Clare: Yes, they were married in 1860 and the next year Lizzie gave birth to a stillborn daughter. Lizzie herself died on 10th February 1862 from an

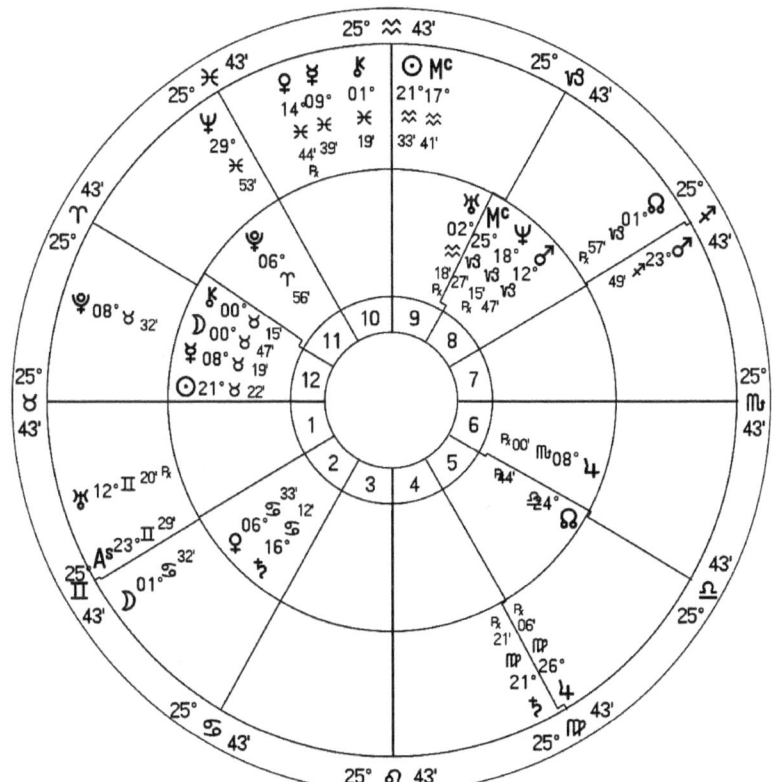

Transits at the time of Lizzie's death – 10 February 1862

overdose of laudenam, an opium-derived drug, following a miscarriage and a bout of severe depression. Overcome with grief and guilt, Rossetti placed the only copy of his complete works of poetry in her coffin, in emulation of a story written by his sister Christina some twelve years previously. Transiting Pluto is at 8° Taurus, exactly on Rossetti's natal Mercury and opposite natal Jupiter, which represents an intensification of the natal T-square. With natal Pluto in Aries square Venus, and transiting Pluto conjunct Mercury and opposite Jupiter, we can understand what led Rossetti to bury, or cast into the underworld, that which he loved and valued most – both Lizzie herself and his poetry. The transit to Mercury not only describes his writing but even suggests the connection with his sister's writing, since Mercury is also the natural planet of siblings.

All of this is an appropriate expression of the Victorian morbid fascination with death, and it makes that painting of Ophelia quite prophetic, doesn't it? There is often a rather fated, doomed, quality about the women in the pre-Raphaelite paintings, as tragic victims of love, laden with grief and guilt.

The solar return for 1861 is revealing and rather painful to read. The Sun-Venus conjunction is isolated in the first house, indicating that Rossetti was rather dissociated, self-absorbed and focusing only on himself, unable to take in the events of that year. The rulers of the seventh house, which would describe Lizzie, and the fifth house of children – the stillbirth and the miscarriage – tell the rest of the story. Both rulers are tightly conjunct in the twelfth house of loss, and the co-ruler of the seventh, Mars in Gemini, is tightly semi-square the Mercury-Pluto conjunction, indicating the extreme mental anguish which led Lizzie to take the overdose. The Sun-Venus conjunction makes no aspects to the rulers of the seventh and fifth houses. The equally isolated and almost exact Chiron-Saturn opposition across the tenth and fourth family houses, indicates loneliness, loss and grief.

Following Lizzie's death, Rossetti leased a house in Cheyne Walk, Chelsea, where he gradually became more of a recluse, surrounding himself with extravagant furnishings and a parade of exotic birds and animals. He began to suffer from headaches and became increasingly addicted to chloral hydrate, which he took to cure his insomnia. But he continued painting and writing poetry and gained sufficient patrons to

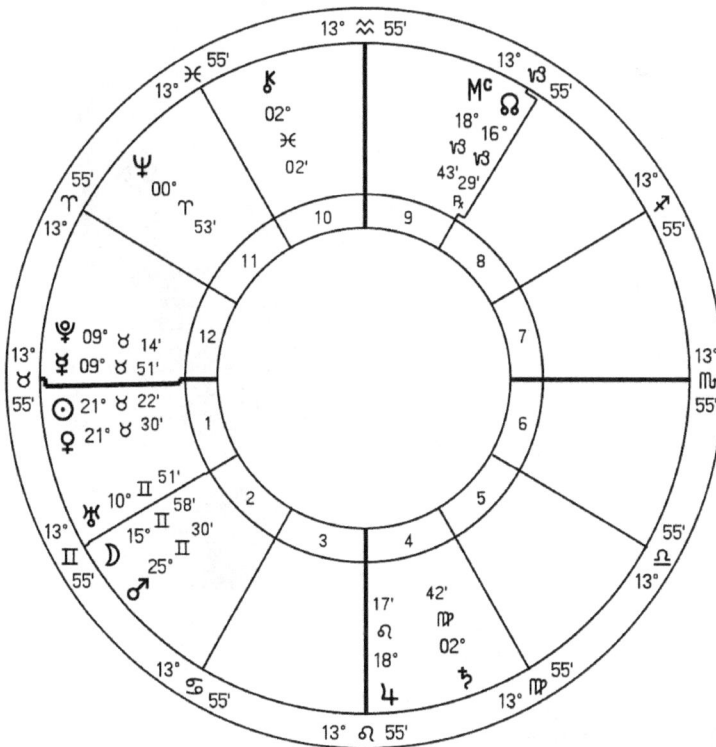

Rossetti – Solar Return for 1861

become relatively prosperous. Another of his models, Fanny Cornforth, became his mistress and housekeeper.

In 1870, after much soul-searching, Rossetti had the body of Elizabeth exhumed in order to retrieve his poetry, much of which was subsequently published. The solar eclipse in Leo at the end of June 1870 was exactly square Rossetti's Sun and picked up his Venus-Pluto square by semi-square and sesqui-quadrate.

Audience: This is getting more morbid all the time.

Clare: In the solar return chart for 1870, Mars is at 8° Taurus, in the same position that Pluto was when Lizzie died, exactly conjunct Mercury and opposite Jupiter in Scorpio. So he buried Lizzie and his poetry when Pluto was on Mercury and exhumed her nine years later when

Mars was on Mercury. Remember that the Chiron transits will carry the natal Chiron-Moon theme, and you can see that Chiron and Venus are conjunct Rossetti's natal Pluto. Transiting Uranus is now exactly opposite Neptune, which can be interpreted as the rather gruesome bringing to light (Uranus) of that which has been lost (Neptune), and Saturn has just entered the eighth house.

It was around this time that Rossetti painted Lizzie once again, as a vision of Dante's muse Beatrice at the precise moment of her death. And this picture illustrates clearly his mental and emotional condition at the time. This is the famous *Beata Beatrix* – a painting with many layers of meaning, representing both Beatrice and Lizzie. It portrays the mystical translation of Beatrice from earth to heaven, a subject taken from Dante's *Vita Nuova*. On the right stands Dante himself, staring across at the Angel of Love, dressed in red and holding a flame. Beatrice sits beside a sundial on which the shadow falls on nine, the hour of her death on 9th June 1290. The red dove, a messenger of love, drops a white poppy, the symbol of sleep, into her folded hands. The poppy is the source of laudanum, the cause of Lizzie's death.

Two years later, in the summer of 1872, and shortly after a solar eclipse which fell directly on his Moon-Chiron conjunction, Rossetti suffered a complete mental and physical breakdown, experiencing hallucinations and hearing accusing voices. The savage reaction of critics to his first collection of poetry was no doubt a contributing factor. He attempted suicide and, although he gradually recovered and was able to paint again, his health continued to deteriorate.

During the period of his breakdown, Pluto was transiting Rossetti's Sun.

The solar return chart for 1872 has Scorpio rising and five planets in the sixth house of health, including both chart rulers – Mercury, Venus, Pluto, Sun and Mars. There is a tight Pluto-Sun-Mars conjunction, Mercury is conjunct natal Chiron and there is a Jupiter-Uranus conjunction on the natal IC. Saturn is conjunct natal Neptune and the Moon is opposite natal Mars.

In 1871 Rossetti and William Morris leased a house together, Kelmscott Manor in Oxfordshire. Jane Morris, William and their two children as well as Rossetti all lived there.

Portrait of Dante Gabriel Rossetti c. 1871, by George Frederic Watts

Jane became Rossetti's main model during that time, and his obsession with her is clear from his paintings. I am sure you are familiar with Rossetti's beautiful paintings of Jane as Persephone, Queen of the Underworld, of which Rossetti painted eight versions. Once again, the theme is symbolically significant, since Persephone was the reluctant wife of Pluto, Hades. In other words, she was a woman in an unhappy marriage.

Audience: It looks really creepy. Was he having an affair with her?

Clare: That's a good question, but I'm not sure anyone actually knows what happened. But we can certainly say, from looking at these pictures, that he was obsessed with her.

Audience: There is something really distorted and uncomfortable about Rossetti's approach to love.

Clare: Yes, and remember that he was born with a tight Pluto-Venus square, so of course he is fascinated by the idea of women and the underworld, with women who are both vulnerable and strong. But Jane was stronger than Lizzie, and a survivor.

Audience: What did William Morris make of all this?

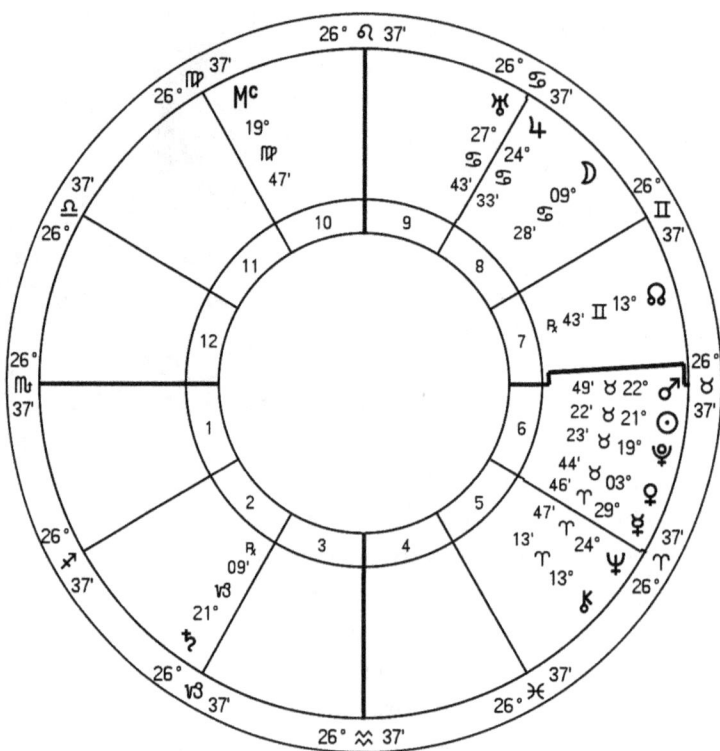

Rossetti – Solar Return Chart 1872

Clare: Well, he was working extremely hard in London at the time, establishing a large enterprise manufacturing prints, fabrics and furniture. Rossetti, his supposed business partner, was ailing, living in Oxfordshire with his wife, and not doing any work. When the lease on Kelmscott Manor was renewed in 1874, Morris wrote Rossetti out of the business partnership and out of the property. He spent the remaining years of his life as a recluse at Cheyne Walk, where he sank into a morbid state, darkened by his addiction to chloral hydrate and subject to increasing mental instability.

Rossetti finally died of kidney failure on 9th April 1882 at the age of 54, at the country house of a friend, where he had gone in a vain attempt to recover his health. He is buried at Birchington-on-Sea, Kent, where his grave is visited by admirers of his life's work and achievements as seen by fresh flowers placed there regularly.

Transiting Chiron was conjunct his Sun and a transiting Jupiter-Pluto conjunction has just crossed his Ascendant, heralding, perhaps, Rossetti's own journey into the underworld.

Notes
1. Alighieri Dante, born in Florence, Italy on 6 June 1265 at 4.33 AM LMT.

LESSON 9

Symbolic Timing Techniques: Secondary Progressions

We are now going to look at the two most popular symbolic timing techniques, secondary progressions and solar arc directions. These techniques are not derived from the actual, outer movement of the planets, but from the birth chart itself.

Secondary progressions trace the organic unfolding of our natal pattern, the changing landscape of our inner world. They are not about outer events or achievements. They are more subtle and internal than that, and basically lunar, with the Moon being the main focus of progressions. By contrast, directions, which we will be looking at next week, are basically solar, and therefore more conscious, since it is the Sun's movement which sets the pace for the development of the entire chart.

Progressions

Progressions can be defined as the actual movement of the planets, before or after birth symbolically related to a specific time period.

There are several different ways of progressing a chart, but this term we are simply going to explore the technique of direct secondary progressions, in which one day of real time is symbolically equivalent to one year of life. So if you look in the ephemeris for the day you were born and then look at the next day, then you will find the progressed positions of the planets when you were one year old. You can easily find your secondary progressions at, say, the age of 37 by counting on 37 days in the ephemeris from the date of your birth. Direct secondary progressions are the most commonly used of the progression techniques and they are very interesting indeed.

So there is an important difference between the interpretation of transits and progressions. Transits are opportunities for us to learn about ourselves as we engage with the outside world – with events and relationships. They trace the external movement of the planets in

Symbolic Timing Techniques: Secondary Progressions 149

external time/space. Their positions are recorded in the ephemeris and they are the same for all of us, although they may or may not affect us personally, since that depends on our natal chart.

Secondary progressions, on the other hand, do not describe the world impinging on us; rather, they describe inner shifts in our thoughts, feelings and attitudes which gradually unfold as the energy contained within each birth chart is released at the rate of one day per year. And of course, it is our changing attitude and approach which will be reflected back to us by the outer world and occasionally, but not always, manifest in the form of events. This is a subtle but important difference because it means that our interpretation of transits will be different from our interpretation of progressions. Hopefully this makes sense to you?

Audience: But we are still basically the same person, with the same birth chart?

Clare: Yes, all forecasting techniques are based on the natal chart and in fact don't make any sense without the natal chart. And all forecasting techniques describe the potential for personal development and evolution during our lifetimes.

Audience: So for each year of life, every planet moves forwards one day. I am 43, so that means that I count down 43 days in the ephemeris from the day I was born and that gives me the positions of my progressed planets?

Clare: Yes, that's right.

Audience: You mentioned that we are going to be using direct secondary progressions. Can you say something about the other techniques for progressing a chart?

Clare: In astrology there are three different types of motion – primary, secondary and tertiary. Primary motion describes the rotation of the Earth on its axis, secondary motion describes the Earth's annual orbit around the Sun, and tertiary motion describes the Moon's orbit around the Earth.

In secondary progressions, one actual year of life is said to be symbolically equivalent to one day in the ephemeris – which is a solar measurement. In tertiary progressions, one month of life is equal to one day in the ephemeris – a lunar measurement, so 36 months, or three years, is equal to 36 in the ephemeris. Primary motion is very technical, since it is measured along the equator, the circle of the Earth's axial rotation, and not the ecliptic. In primary motion, one year of life is equated to the time taken for one degree of right ascension to move across the meridian, which is roughly four minutes of sidereal, or star, time. But you will be glad to hear that we are not going to go there this term.

Audience: How can these progressions possibly work?

Clare: Our premise is that all cycles have the same meaning, no matter what their scale and no matter whether they are astronomically derived or symbolic, so we can say that the cycles of a day and a month and a year, and any other time period, have the same inherent meaning and can be compared to each other. Now, just to make things more complicated, or interesting, progressions can be cast backwards in time as well as forwards, so that in converse secondary progressions one year of life is symbolically equivalent to one day before birth in the ephemeris, and so on, and in converse tertiary progressions, one month of life is equal to one day before birth in the ephemeris, and so on.

Audience: Are forward-moving progressions more positive than converse progressions?

Clare: No, they are not qualitatively different. Rather, they are based on the idea that time unfolds backwards as well as forwards from any given point – in this case from the birth chart. So this means that progressions read backwards are just as meaningful as progressions read forwards. In other words, reverse progressions are based on the assumption that all the progressions we will experience during our entire lives have already been laid down during the last three months of our gestation in the womb (90 days before birth equals 90 years after birth). But whether we

Symbolic Timing Techniques: Secondary Progressions   151

use direct or converse progressions, they both describe the unfolding of our natal charts at the rate of a day for a year.

Audience: So if you are calculating the progressions for the age of 15, they will give you the same information whether you go forwards or backwards in time by 15 days? Like a mirror?

Clare: Yes, good. The converse progressions may add another layer of meaning to the direct progressions. The point here is that our astrological art is fundamentally concerned with the relative nature of time, and it is useful for us to loosen up the conventional understanding of time as a one-directional linear unit of measurement, because we all know that does not really reflect our actual lived experience.

Let's go back to our direct secondary progressions, which describe the unfolding of our natal chart on an internal level. We could use the analogy of the gradual loosening of a coiled spring, because all the energy is already there in our birth chart, and as it unfolds at the rate of one day every year, our attitudes, feelings and thoughts gradually shift on an inner, subjective level. Progressions relate entirely to our natal chart, but they do bring profound change, and we can of course feel quite different in different chapters and phases of our life. And as our inner landscape and attitudes change, that will naturally affect our outer circumstances, so progressions are in a sense the reverse of transits, which we usually experience as outer circumstances impinging on our personal lives.

Another way of thinking about secondary progressions is in terms of entelechy – tracing the organic evolution and changing shape of our inbuilt pattern through time. We could say, for example, that the entelechy of an apple tree is to bud, blossom, flower and bear fruit. An apple tree is only dependent upon the outside world to the extent that it needs the right environment to support its natural development – fertile soil, enough sunlight, etc.

As human beings, however, we have the ability to cooperate with this process consciously, and this is the most important point about the use of progressions. If we co-operate creatively with our inherent inner timing, this will greatly enrich the way we live our lives.

Audience: Can you give us an example, Clare?

Clare: Let's use the progressed Moon as an example, since this moves relatively quickly around our charts, at around 1° a month. The progressed Moon describes our inner feelings and, rather than being unconsciously and blindly subject to our changing emotions and moods, we can use this knowledge to help us ride our emotional waves in a more positive and creative way. Say your progressed Moon has recently moved into Aries, then you are likely to feel more energetic and goal oriented and will instinctively feel that the time has come to take action. If we are aware that our progressed Moon is now in Aries, we can choose to cooperate with this phase and make the most of it, knowing that it will only be in Aries for two and a half years. We have permission, if you like, to take independent action and to drive forwards towards our goals, and indeed if we do not listen to our instincts then we could experience this as a time of increased frustration and anger.

Audience: So transits are more about events, and progressions are more about approach and attitude?

Clare: Exactly, and it is helpful to keep this differentiation in mind when we are interpreting charts. Let's have a look at the average planetary speeds by secondary progression, compared to the average transit time of the planets:

	TRANSIT Daily Motion	SECONDARY PROGRESSION Yearly Motion
SUN	Average 1° degree per day	1° degree per year
MOON	11°47' – 15°12' per day	11°47' – 15°12' per year Approximately 1° per month
MERCURY	Maximum speed 2° per day Goes ℞ 3 times a year, slowing down considerably before changing direction.	Maximum speed 2° per year
VENUS	Maximum speed 1°12' per day Goes ℞ no more than once a year, and some years not at all. Slows down considerably before changing direction	Maximum speed 1°12' per year

Symbolic Timing Techniques: Secondary Progressions

MARS	30' – 40' a day Goes ℞ approximately every two years. Slows down considerably before changing direction	30' – 40' a year
JUPITER	Maximum 14' per day Goes ℞ once a year for as long as 4 months	Maximum 14' per year
SATURN	Maximum 7' per day Goes ℞ once a year for as long as 5 months	Maximum 7' per year
URANUS	2 – 5' per day Goes ℞ once a year for more than 5 months	2 – 5' per year
NEPTUNE	Maximum 2' per day Goes ℞ once a year for more than 5 months	Maximum 2' per year
PLUTO	Maximum 2' per day Goes ℞ once a year for more than 5 months	Maximum 2' per year

This table tells us some interesting things about progressions. The Sun moves roughly one degree a year, and the Moon moves roughly one degree a month, completing its progressed journey right around the chart every 28 years. If you live to be 90 years old, this means that the Sun will progress about 90° or through three signs of the zodiac, whereas the Moon will progress more than three times right around the chart. Generally speaking, when we are studying progressions, the angles and the planets out to Mars are given the most attention.

Audience: And transits are used more for the outer planets?

Clare: Yes, from Mars outwards. This helps us to refine our forecasting work, which would otherwise be far too unwieldy. But it is always worth checking all the planets for changes of direction.

Audience: Can you explain why this is important, Clare?

Clare: It is always important when a planet changes direction by progression. Firstly, that planet slows down considerably and becomes stationary, which means that it will exert a much more powerful force on the natal chart. The stations of Mercury and Venus can last for several years and the stations of Neptune and Pluto can last an entire lifetime. Secondly, when a planet changes direction, our relationship to that planet will change. When a natally direct planet turns retrograde its expression becomes more internalised, reflective and thoughtful. And when a natally retrograde planet turns direct it will start to express itself in a more overt and uninhibited way, but with an increased level of confidence, maturity and depth which it has gained during the retrograde period.

It is definitely worth checking the actual speed of the planets at the time of your birth, which will give you a good idea of the power of their influence in your chart.

Audience: Can I ask something? My progressed Chiron doesn't appear to have moved at all. It has gone one degree back. And Saturn has gone two degrees forward. Can that be right?

Clare: Yes of course it can. Let's look at that. When you were born, Saturn must have been moving forwards quite fast, so your Saturn has moved two degrees forwards in your lifetime. Had you been born when Saturn was stationary, it might not have moved at all by progression. As far as Chiron is concerned, have a look at the ephemeris and you will probably find that it was changing direction when you were born, which would explain why it hasn't moved at all. Planets are changing speed all the time, sometimes going quickly and sometimes slowing down before changing direction. This is much more obvious when we are working with progressions than when we are working with transits.

WORKING WITH PROGRESSIONS

There are two main ways of working with progressions – one is to study the progressed chart itself, in its own terms, and the other is to compare the progressed chart with the natal chart. There are some key factors to look for, and I have put these into a list which you can use as a quick guide when you are working with progressions.

Progressions Check List

1. Progressed Moon sign and natal house
2. Progressed Lunar Cycle and Lunation Phase
3. Progressed Sun, by sign and natal house
4. Progressed Angles – MC & ASC – by sign and natal house
5. Progressed planets changing direction
6. Progressed Aspects – gradually tightening up or loosening

Symbolic Timing Techniques: Secondary Progressions   155

Progressed Moon
The progressed Moon moves approximately one degree a month and spends two and a half years in each sign, and in each house, if we use the Equal house system. As the progressed Moon changes sign and natal house our feelings and emotional responses will change accordingly and we will be emotionally involved and experience changes in the area of life described by the house it is currently progressing through. As I mentioned before, following our progressed Moon's journey around the chart encourages us to validate our feelings and instincts for a particular period of time. This is a very creative and self-nurturing way to work, since of all the planets, it is usually our Moon's needs which we most ignore, abuse or deny.

So, for example, if the Moon is progressing through Gemini, then we might be enjoying our freedom and instinctively resist making any serious or long term commitments. But when the Moon progresses into Cancer, we might start to feel that the time has come to move house or settle down, which is quite a different feeling.

Audience: When my progressed Moon moved from Taurus to Gemini, it was a few months before the focus shifted and I started enjoying what I was doing.

Clare: Did you feel more light-hearted?

Audience: Yes, I started to take things less seriously and to have some fun.

Audience: Darby (Costello) says that you should never buy any clothes when the progressed Moon is at 29 degrees of a sign, because you will end up not wearing them!

Clare: Exactly. And I think it is fairly common for people to consult an astrologer when they sense an inner shift, so it is always worth checking the progressions because then we can help them understand what is going on in their inner landscape.

Audience: That is very helpful because I have progressed Moon in Cancer at the moment and I just feel like staying at home and going nowhere. But my partner is always wanting us to go out and socialise.

Clare: This is a good example because, if you are going to be true to your instincts, then you will be feeling self protective and home-centred for now. Perhaps you could explain to your partner that this is just how you feel at the moment, and that you will certainly start feeling like having some fun and being more sociable when your Moon progresses into Leo. Do you know how many degrees your progressed Moon is at the moment?

Audience: Yes, it is at 24°.

Clare: So perhaps you can give yourself permission to nurture yourself for the next six months, knowing that you will start to feel quite different when your Moon progresses into Leo.

Audience: I have just had my progressed Moon in Capricorn, which was a kind of lonely and inward looking and hard working time for me. But I was able to really get down to my writing, and now my Moon has progressed into Aquarius I am all over the place. I wish I had used that time better, so I can quite appreciate that we need to use our progressed Moons.

Audience: How does the Moon in Virgo feel?

Clare: When the Moon progresses into Virgo, we might well feel that it is time to get organised, sort things out and pay more attention to our health and diet. We may be feeling more industrious, or that it is time to develop some more skills.

Progressed Moon Cycle

Clare: The progressed Moon takes about 27–28 years to go round the chart, so in a lifetime we will experience two or three complete cycles. This cycle is age dependent, which means that we all get the same progressed Moon phases at the same age.

Symbolic Timing Techniques: Secondary Progressions

Progressed Moon's aspects to Natal Moon	1st Progressed Moon Cycle Approx Age	2nd Progressed Moon Cycle Approx Age
☽p □ ☽n	6.7	32.4
☽p ☍ ☽n	13 – 15	Early 40s
☽p □ ☽n	21	48 - 49
☽p ☌ ☽n	27.5	54.5 – 55

Audience: What does it mean when your Moon comes back to join the natal Moon?

Clare: That is known as a progressed lunar return, which means that we have completed a whole cycle of emotional experience and that we are about to begin another one. Whenever a cycle repeats, it will bring up memories of the previous cycle, so the progressed Moon position may well be stirring deep memories of the past from 27–28 years ago, and it is always worth checking back to see what was happening last time. Both for ourselves and for our clients, this is an opportunity to revisit past feelings and to do some further emotional processing, now that we have the additional perspective of another lunation cycle.

Audience: It is interesting that you say this, Clare, because I have been thinking a lot about my father recently, and he died almost 28 years ago, so my progressed Moon must be back where it was when he died?

Clare: That's right, and you may well be having dreams about him, as if your psyche is drawing him to your attention. And your memories of him may change as a result. This is an excellent example of the way that our emotional processing continues throughout our lives, as the progressed Moon continues to revisit the past.

It is also worth noting that the lunation cycle is slightly shorter in length than the transiting Saturn cycle, and the relationship between these two cycles is particularly strong during the first 28 years of our lives. This tells us that our emotional development (progressed Moon) and our experiences of the world (transiting Saturn) are particularly closely linked in our early years. Both cycles evoke memories of the past, offering us an opportunity to re-engage with and resolve any unfinished business, so that we can move forwards. These two cycles gradually drift apart by up to five and seven years respectively by the time of the second and third progressed lunar returns.

The Progressed Lunation Cycle
Another way of analyzing the progressed Moon is to study its changing relationship to the progressed Sun, and this is known as the progressed lunation cycle, which is approximately 30 years long. We have already looked at the way that cycles unfold and we have already discovered our natal lunar type, which is an expression of the relationship between the Sun and Moon when we were born. Our lunar type is personal, and not age-dependent.

The nearest new Moon prior to birth will have initiated a new lunar cycle, and every natal chart will reflect the relationship between the Sun and Moon at a particular stage in the lunar cycle that began before birth. At some point during the first 30 years of our lives we will experience the first new Moon phase of our progressed lunation cycle, an important seed moment, setting the scene for the following 30-year cycle.

We have already looked at the eight lunation phases defined by Dane Rudhyar, and it is very useful to follow the progressed Moon around the chart, both in terms of the natal houses and signs it is progressing through, but also in terms of the eight phases in this thirty-year cycle. This enables us to cooperate with the tidal effect of the progressed lunation cycle, growing and expanding during the waxing phase, and giving out and sharing what has been achieved or realized during the more mellow, mature waning phase. The eight phases of the progressed lunation cycle follow exactly the same energetic pattern as the monthly transiting Moon cycle, but slowed down considerably. So their interpretation will be the same, but of course they will be more internal, to do with our inner pattern. A new lunation cycle indicates a new chapter in our lives, a new seed to be nurtured, the seed moment being the sign and house in which the new lunation cycle occurs. As before, this cycle will take root at the progressed first quarter, which occurs seven and a half years later, and we will gain objectivity and detachment at the progressed full Moon, 14 years later. Re-orientation and realism will be needed 22 years later, at the progressed last quarter, after which the cycle begins to run out of steam, as it were, letting go and preparing for the next progressed lunation cycle.

I am going to present you with a case study later, which should bring all this to life, but it is certainly worth tracing your own progressed lunation cycle and seeing when it started and in what natal sign and house, and where you are on that cycle at the moment. As with all progressions, this is an inner process and only you will really be able to know what this feels like on the inside.

Progressed Sun
The next most important progression is that of the Sun, which is always identical to the position of the solar arc directed Sun, which we will look at next week. Because the Sun moves about one degree a year, it will change sign and house – in the Equal house system – every 30 years or so, heralding a shift in our consciousness, a new inner identity and a new kind of creative self expression. The qualities of the next sign or house seek expression and we will find that our attitudes and responses will change accordingly. We can usually remember when our Sun's changed signs by progression and direction.

Audience: Presumably it takes a while for us to feel the change? I don't think I felt it for a while, but I can see the shift more clearly with hindsight.

Clare: Well, we are all creatures of habit, so of course it can take a while for the old patterns to change.

Audience (Laura): My natal Sun is at 28° Aquarius so it would have gone into Pisces when I was two years old, and I used to be extremely quiet and shy. Now that my progressed Sun is in Aries, no one can believe I was ever shy.

Clare: When the progressed Sun changes sign, it will change its polarity, modality and element. For 30 years your inner Sun in Pisces was negative, mutable and watery, but when you were 32 your inner Sun shifted to Aries and became positive, cardinal and fiery. Quite a difference, but remember that this is an internal shift. It is likely that you would have started to feel more focused and determined, with more clarity and energy. Your natal Aquarian Sun is now supported by a progressed Sun which is more assertive, active and courageous.

Audience (Laura): So I am still an Aquarius Sun but in an Arian sort of way?

Clare: Yes. Aries is spontaneous, courageous and goal orientated – to do with personal survival. Progressed Sun in Aries will provide a background of focus and determination and the personal inner resources to support your humanitarian, idealistic Aquarian Sun. It is the Sun in the natal chart which describes our journey towards conscious self expression, and the progressed Sun describes our inner attitude, a particular aspect of solar energy which is accessible to us for a period of time. It comes from within.

Audience (Laura): This is really interesting because I think of myself as really Neptunian and over-sensitive. My Mercury and Venus are in Pisces and I have always felt too vulnerable. But you are right that I did start to identify with the warrior archetype when I was in my early 30s, and I remember being rather surprised. That was when I read Joseph Campbell's *Hero with a Thousand Faces* and other books about warriors. I remember consciously deciding to quit being such a wimp and to become tougher and more assertive.

Clare: The important word here is 'consciously', because we are talking about the Sun here and that is a solar word. You may have lost your sense of yourself to some extent when your Sun was progressing through Pisces and then something changed.

Audience (Laura): Yes, I had had enough of all that.

Clare: That feeling of having had enough is exactly the kind of inner shift of attitude which progressions indicate. Nevertheless, your experience of progressed Sun in Pisces will undoubtedly leave a legacy of sensitivity and compassion, which also has its value. You mentioned that you have natal Mercury and Venus in Pisces, which means that your progressed

Symbolic Timing Techniques: Secondary Progressions   161

Sun would have crossed over these at some point, focusing attention of the expression of those natal planets.

Audience (Laura): Something really weird just occurred to me, which happened when I was 32. Can I tell it?

Clare: Sure.

Audience (Laura): I was having a really bad time then. I had been attacked outside my house and was very traumatised. I became agoraphobic and was on pills and could not leave my house. And then I remember thinking, right I am not taking this any more, I am not hiding away, and that happened when my Sun progressed into Aries. I remember I tried to make myself go out and start doing things again. And it happened that there was this guy I knew who was really fiery, strong and powerful and I would pretend to be him, thinking: 'OK, what would he do in this situation?' He was my role model and I sort of borrowed his energy. And after all these years I have just found out his birthday, and he has an Aries Sun.

Clare: That's a wonderful example. Is anyone else surprised to find their progressed Sun in a completely different sign?

Audience (Joyce): My progressed Sun is about to go into Scorpio. I think it is 29 degrees Libra at the moment.

Clare: How does that feel?

Audience (Joyce): It is quite funny, actually, because I have always been known at work for being very diplomatic. But recently I have found myself becoming much more intolerant, and unable to put up with the people I work with.

Clare: Scorpio does not suffer fools gladly.

Audience (Joyce): That's right. I do focus groups with consumers, ordinary people, often housewives. There was a time when I could tolerate them but now they drive me up the wall, and I end up shouting at them. And I am getting worried now, because I seem to have lost my patience.

Clare: What benefits could this bring to your work, having the progressed Sun in Scorpio?

Audience (Joyce): Well I suppose it could bring deeper insight. A lot of the stuff I am doing at the moment requires real focus and analysis. Maybe I will do that as well then.

Clare: So you could say that you have been a Libra Sun for 30 years, which brought you into this kind of group work in the first place, finding out what other people think, which is very Libran, but now you are ready to go deeper. None of this means that the Sun in your natal chart has altered, but it is good to understand why you might be feeling more intolerant at the moment. And a great deal more focused. This can be tremendously effective – you can focus your energy in a particular way, exactly where you want it to be. When we are working with astrology we realise that change happens all the time and there is no such thing as staying in the same place. And this is the opening of another layer of experience, which will coexist with your natal pattern.

Audience (Joyce): I suppose that's right, very tactful. So it's about building on past experience.

Clare: Yes, developing further skills as additional aspects of your personality come to life. It is always interesting to watch this shift, and to see Cancerians become Leos and Leos become Virgos by progression, for example.

Audience: Does our approach to relationships change when the progressed ASC/DES axis changes to another sign?

Clare: Absolutely.

Audience (Janet): My natal Sun is at five degrees Scorpio and progressed into Sagittarius when I was 26 – the year I joined the foreign service. I am 51 now and been in the same job since then. I remember thinking at the time that I wanted to travel, and my career goal was to be paid to travel.

Clare: This is an excellent example of how an inner change of orientation leads to change in the outer world. No doubt you sensed that a new chapter was beginning in your life, the focus of which was Sagittarian in its nature, to do with foreign travel. Progressions have a different way of working than transits, we make decisions based on an inner shift of emphasis, which in turn affects our outer lives.

Progressed Mercury
Most of us will experience a change of direction of progressed Mercury at some point during our lives, and this is always significant. If you were born with a retrograde Mercury, for example, which is not particularly uncommon, then it will turn direct at some point during the first 24 years of your life, since by transit it spends a maximum of about 24 days retrograde. When planets change direction, the birth chart begins to change shape from within and there will be an inner change of attitude.

A retrograde Mercury at birth usually describes someone who is naturally more of a listener, absorbing everything in their immediate environment, taking it all in, as it were. When Mercury goes direct by progression, there is a noticeable shift as that individual finds their voice, starts to venture opinions, drawing on everything which has been absorbed until then. And the reverse is also true. When a direct Mercury at birth goes retrograde by progression, this will be the beginning of a more philosophical, contemplative phase of life, an increased focus on one's inner thoughts and an excellent time for processing and sorting what has already been learned. It is important to realize that there is nothing negative about the meaning of a retrograde planet. And when Mercury changes sign by progression, information will be processed in a different way, reflecting the nature of the sign. Has anyone got an example for us to look at?

Audience: Mercury was direct when I was born and went retrograde when I was 36. It only turned direct again a year ago, when I was 54. And I have really noticed a change – my mind is clearer now, and I have also started to study again.

Clare: So your progressed Mercury was retrograde for 18 years and would have been stationary, and therefore very powerful, for about three or four years around the age of 36 when it changed direction. And it is very slow again now, which means that Mercury is particularly emphasised at the moment, since it just changed direction last year. We could say that it is gathering itself now for a new phase of self expression in the outer world.

Progressed Venus
Venus does not go retrograde as often as Mercury, and can be direct for an entire lifetime. When it does go retrograde, it can be for up to 40 days, or 40 years by secondary progression. When Venus changes sign by progression our values will change and we are likely to develop new interests and pleasures. And the way we relate to others will also change.

Audience (Rob): I was born with Venus in Aquarius retrograde. It's in the seventh house conjunct Chiron and opposite Uranus. Could we have a look at that?

Clare: Yes, and first of all we need to find out what your natal Venus wants.

Audience: Freedom and space in relationships?

Audience: Idealistic about relationships?

Audience: Will it be rather detached, with the focus of relationships being on the intellect rather than the emotions?

Audience: Would he want an unconventional relationship?

Clare: Yes, all of the above. Venus in Aquarius values friendship, honesty, equality and openness. And that is supported by the opposition

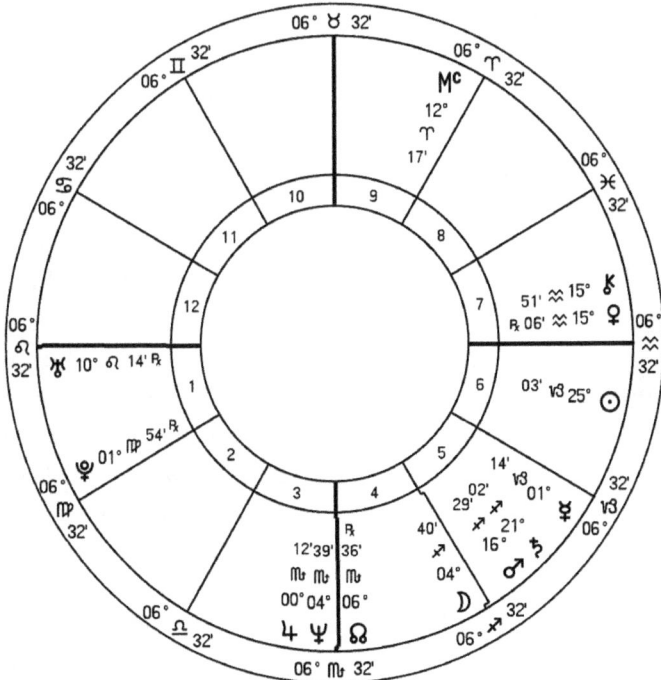

Rob – Progressed Venus 15 Jan 1958, 5.11pm GMT, York

to Uranus. Relationships are not likely to be based on need, but on mutual mental attraction or ideals. I do think this is a detached, friendly kind of Venus. Would you agree with that?

Audience (Rob): Yes. But it is conjunct Chiron.

Clare: This adds another layer of interpretation because it brings Venus together with the Uranus-Chiron opposition, across the relationship axis. So perhaps you feel rather isolated and cut off? Certainly this is friendly at a distance but the question is how to get closer to someone in the face of so much detachment? It is possible that you are very afraid of being abandoned, and this could be a primal experience or memory, so the Venus-Uranus opposition could be used as a defence against getting too close. If we are looking for a wound around relationships, then we might suppose it concerns intimacy?

Audience (Rob): Spot on.

Clare: Let's see if this Venus becomes stationary by progression at some point, and turns direct. That will be an important event. Have a look at the ephemeris.

Audience (Rob): Venus became stationary 33 years after I was born. At 0° Aquarius.

Clare: So Venus was retrograde for the first 33 years of your life, and in fact it opposed your natal Uranus when you were about eleven, when you might have cut off even more, and, because of the natal Chiron-Venus conjunction, you may well have felt inadequate or in some way not good enough, since Venus in the seventh house in Aquarius needs to be recognised and valued by others, and its progression retrograde opposite Uranus indicates an experience of isolation or separation which is likely to have been painful.

Audience (Rob): Well, there was a big change when I was eleven, because I was sent to boarding school, and that was a very bad experience for me. I felt utterly alone and thought there was something wrong with me because it took me ages to make friends.

Clare: If a planet is retrograde natally, then its expression is usually quite introverted. With Venus retrograde at birth, I would imagine that you were already comfortable in your own company and that your pleasures and interests were quite private and self sufficient. But you were separated from your familiar environment at that time and expected to be gregarious and get on with a whole new group of people. After that, Venus would have progressed back over your Descendant and into your sixth house, and then, at the age of 33, Venus became stationary at 0° Aquarius and it is now direct for the first time in your life. I would imagine you have felt a significant shift in your values and in relationships as well. Perhaps you are being drawn towards new groups of people and now feel more expansive and trusting, feeling as if it is safer to reach out a bit?

Audience (Rob): I probably became a bit more creative, and joining this astrology group has been an important step for me. And I think becoming a dad has definitely helped. I am not a naturally trusting person, and I am not proud of that.

Clare: Well, it sounds as if there are good reasons why you have found it difficult to trust, since early wounds take a long time to heal. Nevertheless, now that Venus is moving forwards by progression and will go over your Descendant again, you may become involved in working with others, since this is a seventh house Venus, the house of one-to-one relationships, often professional relationships. As Venus becomes more overt and active, one real possibility with the seventh house Venus-Chiron conjunction would be to work in a healing or caring capacity of some sort. That would be the difference between an introverted Venus and a Venus gradually becoming more extroverted, realising that you have a talent for helping others, no doubt due to the resources developed during that retrograde phase. If your natal Venus had been direct, then it would have moved quickly away from the Chiron and that would be a different thing. But this is a mature Venus which has slowly moved backwards, opposed Uranus and crossed the Descendant, and these are experiences that build inner values and strength.

Progressed Mars
The speed of transiting Mars varies considerably during its two-year orbit. As a superior planet, Mars slows down as it approaches its conjunction with the Sun, when it will be in superior conjunction and at its furthest point from the earth. As Mars moves away from the Sun it will speed up considerably, before slowing down and going retrograde at the Sun-Mars opposition. When it turns direct it will once again speed up as it separates from the opposition. It is always worth checking the speed of Mars, which will give us additional information about its level of activity, assertiveness and drive, and its speed at birth plays a part in this. Mars may be direct our entire lives, but can be retrograde for up to 81 days, or years by secondary progression.

There is a considerable difference in the expression of a direct and retrograde Mars. A direct Mars has an Aries quality, being competitive, assertive and physically energetic. A retrograde Mars has a Scorpio quality, being more subtle, persistent and covert. And of course the quality of that energy will shift if Mars happens to progress into a new sign.

The progressions of the planets from Jupiter outwards are much slower, changing sign and direction far less often than the personal planets. The outer planets spend a significant amount of time retrograde, so generally speaking we would only pay attention to the outer planets if they change direction.

The Progressed Chart
The value of the progressed chart itself is that it gives us a visual picture of the way the natal chart gradually changes shape during our lifetimes. We can watch our natal angles change and our natal aspects and aspect patterns tighten up or loosen.

It is only the angles and the personal planets – Moon, Sun, Mercury, Venus and Mars – which will form new aspects in the progressed chart. For example, an applying natal trine or sextile can tighten and even become exact by progression – in which case there will be a gradual increase in the level of mutual support between the two planets. In the case of an applying natal opposition or square there will be a gradually increasing level of tension and confrontation between the two planets. Or a tight but separating natal opposition or square can loosen during life, gradually easing the inherent tension.

For example, if you were born with Venus at 15° Gemini and Saturn at 18° Virgo, then you were born with a Venus-Saturn square. There are many ways of interpreting this square, but we know that in general it describes a lack of self confidence and a level of inhibition around relationships. Now, assuming that both planets are direct, we know that this square is going to tighten up and become exact by progression, since Venus moves faster than Saturn. So the experience of this square will gradually intensify to the point of exactitude many years later, which may well indicate marriage, signifying commitment in relationships, which is one interpretation of Venus and Saturn, or even the year we get divorced, depending on the circumstances. So that is going to be really significant, but it is an expression of an inner development, rather than something which happens to us 'out of the blue'.

In my own chart I have Mars at 2° Scorpio and Jupiter at 12° Taurus, so they are not in aspect, but since I was born Mars has moved 16° and Jupiter has moved 6°, so they have formed an exact opposition by progression, at 18° Scorpio/Taurus. Do you see that? This opposition has taken all my life to form, but now it is exact. And, since my natal Pluto is at 19° Leo, I now have a progressed fixed T-square by progression, which is extremely focused and determined and feels very different from my natal chart. It is something which has gradually formed from within.

Audience: It is like looking through a kaleidoscope and watching the patterns change.

Clare: That's right, and we can equally find that natal squares or T-squares loosen and become easier, trines and kites emerge or disappear, and yods form or dissolve. In fact you can set your astrological software to see this process for yourselves, and watch the shape of your chart gradually changing.

Audience: I have just noticed that I have several progressed planets in earth, although I have no earth at all in my birth chart.

Clare: So we could say that you are gradually feeling more secure and confident and therefore your attitude is more practical and realistic, since earth signs always follow fire signs.

Audience: Are secondary progressed charts drawn up for the same place you were born?

Clare: Yes, since they describe the inner unfolding of the birth chart itself.

Progressed Angles
The progressed angles are an important part of this changing picture, and so we also need to consider the MC/IC axis and Ascendant/Descendant axis as they progress into different signs, when the quality of our personal orientation to, and interface with, the world will shift. You will see from your software that there are several ways to progress the angles, and you need know about the two most commonly used methods.
 The first is the derived Ascendant method and the second is the solar arc method. In both systems, the MC progresses by one degree of solar

arc each year, which is roughly one degree a year. But the method for calculating the progressed Ascendant is different.

Progressions keep their relationship not only to real time but also to real space, and this means that the different rising times of the signs on the Ascendant need to be taken into consideration. We have already seen how the angle between the two axes is constantly changing. The derived Ascendant is calculated from the progressed MC at the place of birth, and its speed depends on whether you were born with a sign of long or short ascension rising.

So for example, in the northern hemisphere Pisces is a sign of short ascension – which means that it takes about an hour to rise, so your Ascendant will progress more quickly – at around two degrees a year. If, on the other hand, you are born with Virgo rising, which is a sign of long ascension in the northern hemisphere taking about three hours to rise, then the Ascendant will progress more slowly – at around half a degree a year – because it is based on real time at the place of birth, as if it was a real chart, even though it is slowed down to one day for a year.

Audience: Oh no, that means I am going to be stuck with a progressed Virgo Ascendant all my life.

Audience: Can you explain the long and short signs of ascension?

Clare: Simply put, this is to do with the fact that there is an oblique angle between the Earth's plane (celestial equator) and the Sun's plane (ecliptic) – and it is this oblique angle which causes our seasons. Some signs (such as Pisces) rise more obliquely over the eastern horizon and therefore take a shorter time to rise than other signs (such as Virgo) which rise more vertically and therefore take longer to rise. And it is the reverse in the southern hemisphere.

Audience: So that's why so many of my Australian friends have Pisces rising?

Clare: Yes, and of course most of us are born somewhere in the middle of these two extremes, so it is less noticeable. But if you happen to be born in Australia with a Pisces rising chart, then your progressed Ascendant

Symbolic Timing Techniques: Secondary Progressions

could remain in Pisces all your life. Conversely, if you are born in the northern hemisphere with Pisces rising, then you could go through two or even three progressed Ascendants in your lifetime.

The solar arc method of progressing the angles is not derived from the place of birth. Solar arc angles simply add the solar arc distance travelled in a day to both the MC and Ascendant each year, so the relationship between the natal angles remains the same. Over time, the derived and solar arc Ascendants usually grow apart, but whichever method we use it makes sense to stick to our general interpretation rules. The derived Ascendant belongs naturally to the progressed chart, describing our changing attitude to the world, and the solar arc Ascendant belongs naturally to the directed chart, which is more likely to manifest as external events.

Audience (Tessa): My natal Midheaven is in Aries but it progressed into Taurus when I was 24 and it is now at 20° Taurus, the focal point of a progressed yod with Venus at 20° Libra, which has progressed 27 degrees and Saturn at 20° Sagittarius, which has progressed 2 degrees since I was born. In my natal chart there are no aspects between Venus, Saturn and the Midheaven.

Clare: So you now have this finger of fate pointing to your progressed Midheaven, your life direction, and it has taken your entire life for this aspect pattern to form. I would imagine there is something of an artistic or financial nature you feel ready to achieve, since Saturn is involved and Venus is the ruler of your progressed Midheaven. This is your opportunity to give shape to something which is of value to you. To use the progressed Venus-Saturn sextile to give shape to your artistic expression. This is important right now. Not last year or next year, but now.

Audience (Tessa): That is so right because I have been writing a book for a few years but I really feel that this is the time to get it finished. But will the yod only be like this for a year?

Clare: Yes because next year your progressed Midheaven will be 21° Taurus, Venus will have moved on, and you will have lost the yod and with it the career focus. This is another example of how we can creatively use astrological kairos and seize the moment.

Audience: Do you look at progressed planets changing house in the natal chart or in the progressed chart?

Clare: I think it gets very complicated indeed if you start to use the progressed houses. Generally, it is simpler to look at the progressed planets changing houses in the natal chart, otherwise we start to lose our connection to the natal chart.

Audience: And when a progressed planet hits a natal planet?

Clare: As always, we need to assess the natal meaning of the planet which is progressing, because it is the progressed planet which is 'acting upon' the natal planet. Say Mercury is in Pisces natally and then it progresses into Aries and onto a planet in Aries – say the Sun. Its core expression will always be Piscean, but now it seeks to express itself in a more pioneering, goal-oriented way. So, for example, that individual may be thinking about starting a new poetry group or even swimming group. It is not just any old Mercury progressing into Aries and onto the natal Aries Sun – it is a Piscean Mercury.

Audience: How do you decide which techniques to use? Do you use them all?

Audience: In his *Horoscope Symbols*, Rob Hand writes that techniques are like tools in a toolbox. We need to make a commitment to one or two tools and use them properly, rather than using a bit of one tool and a bit of another, trying to get something to fit. You have to use the whole tool or you end up with a mess.

Clare: Yes, and the same debate is going on in integrative psychotherapy at the moment. Integrative does not mean eclectic. If you have an integrative approach you still have to have a fundamental philosophy that holds together. Whatever techniques different astrologers use, I think we all accept that there is a fundamental relationship between 'cosmos

Symbolic Timing Techniques: Secondary Progressions 173

and psyche'. All our techniques are ways of studying that relationship from a series of different philosophical and practical viewpoints.

Audience: Presumably they are all different layers of analysis and throw up different levels of meaning.

Progressions Case Study

Now that we know something about our case study, and have traced some of the most significant transits, I want to show you how Rossetti's chart developed by progression throughout his lifetime.

First of all, let's look at the progressed chart at the time of his death, so that we can see visually how the natal chart has changed shape.

Using orbs of 1° only, you can see clearly how the shape of Rossetti's chart has changed by progression. He has lost the tight Mercury-Jupiter opposition, and Mercury has progressed into the first house and into Leo, where it is in an applying trine to Pluto and in an applying conjunction to Venus, also in the first house and in Leo. He has gained the personal fame and recognition he sought and made a significant and lasting contribution to art and poetry. The natal Mars-Pluto square has now become exact, with Mars retrograde by progression.

Turning to the progressed Moon, Rossetti was only 54 when he died, so the Moon has nearly competed two cycles and is about to progress into Rossetti's natal twelfth house. The progressed chart reveals an important T-square, with the nodal axis square Saturn, and the progressed Moon, which would have been exactly on the south node and square Saturn the previous month just beginning to separate from this configuration.

In addition, the progressed nodal axis is now applying to square the progressed Ascendant-Descendant axis, which itself is forming an alignment with progressed Saturn. We could say that this T-square had been brought into emotional prominence the previous month by the progressed Moon.

Audience: How would you interpret that?

Clare: I wouldn't actually want to look for events in the secondary progressions, but by this time, Rossetti knew he was dying and the involvement of the nodal axis in this T-square does seem to have an inevitability and finality about it. In the end he died of consumption

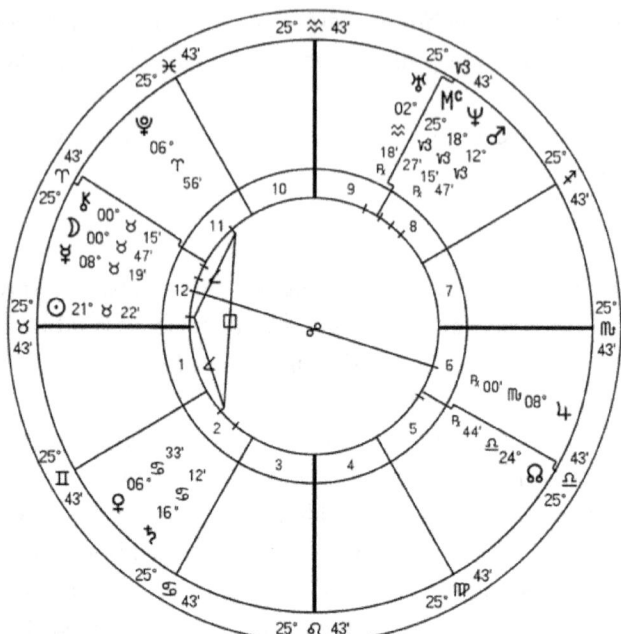

Rossetti – Natal Chart

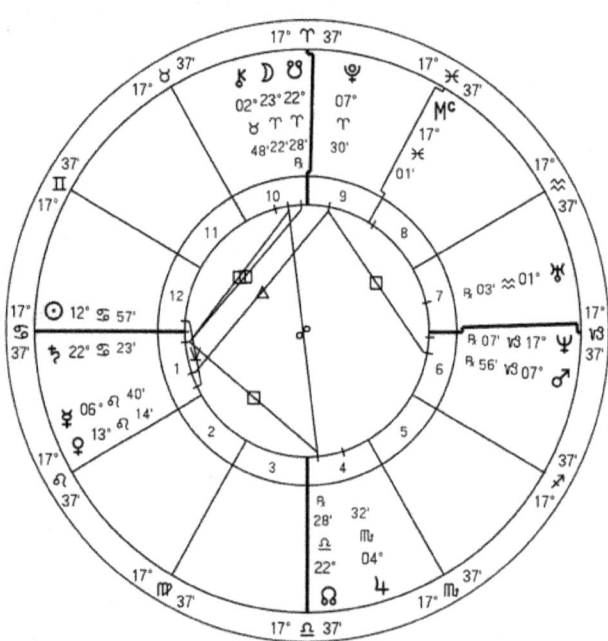

Rossetti – Natal Chart Progressed to Date of Death

Symbolic Timing Techniques: Secondary Progressions   175

and finally kidney failure – but basically it was his addictions which had gradually weakened him.

It is never easy when Saturn squares the nodal axis either natally, by transit or by progression. The progressions describe Rossetti's inner landscape at the time, and we can imagine his feelings of loneliness, isolation and even despair. Remember that it has taken 54 years – Rossetti's entire life – for this complex progressed T-square to progress into exactitude, with the nodal axis moving retrograde just over 3° and Saturn progressing 6°, joined by the progressed Moon in Aries in its last quarter phase.

The Sun has progressed from Taurus, through Gemini and into Cancer around twelve years previously. It is now directly opposite Rossetti's natal eighth house Mars, indicating a struggle for survival, as does his progressed Moon in Aries.

Graphic Ephemeris

I want to introduce you to the graphic ephemeris, which is a splendid forecasting tool and one you can easily generate from your software. A computer generated chart gives us a static picture which, however useful as an accurate map of a moment in time/space, obscures the fact that each chart is the expression of dynamic movement, caught in one moment. Each chart is part of an ever-changing bigger picture and if we are to see that bigger picture then our scale needs to be bigger too.

It is extremely useful to use a printed or graphic ephemeris when you are working with progressions because you can see visually how a birth chart unfolds during a lifetime. The natal patterns gradually shift, and you can see at a glance the changing relationship of the planets to each other, how the planets gradually slow down, become stationary and start moving in the opposite direction, and when both the planets and angles progress into new signs.

Let's have a look at Rossetti's lifetime progressions. These will tell us how his inner landscape changes. This graphic ephemeris is set for 54 years, from 1st May 1828 to 1st May 1882, as you can see on the horizontal axis.

There are three vertical columns on the left-hand side of the page listing the degrees of all the cardinal, fixed and mutable signs respectively. On the right-hand side of the page you will see the birth positions

176 Mapping the Psyche 3: Kairos – The Astrology of Time

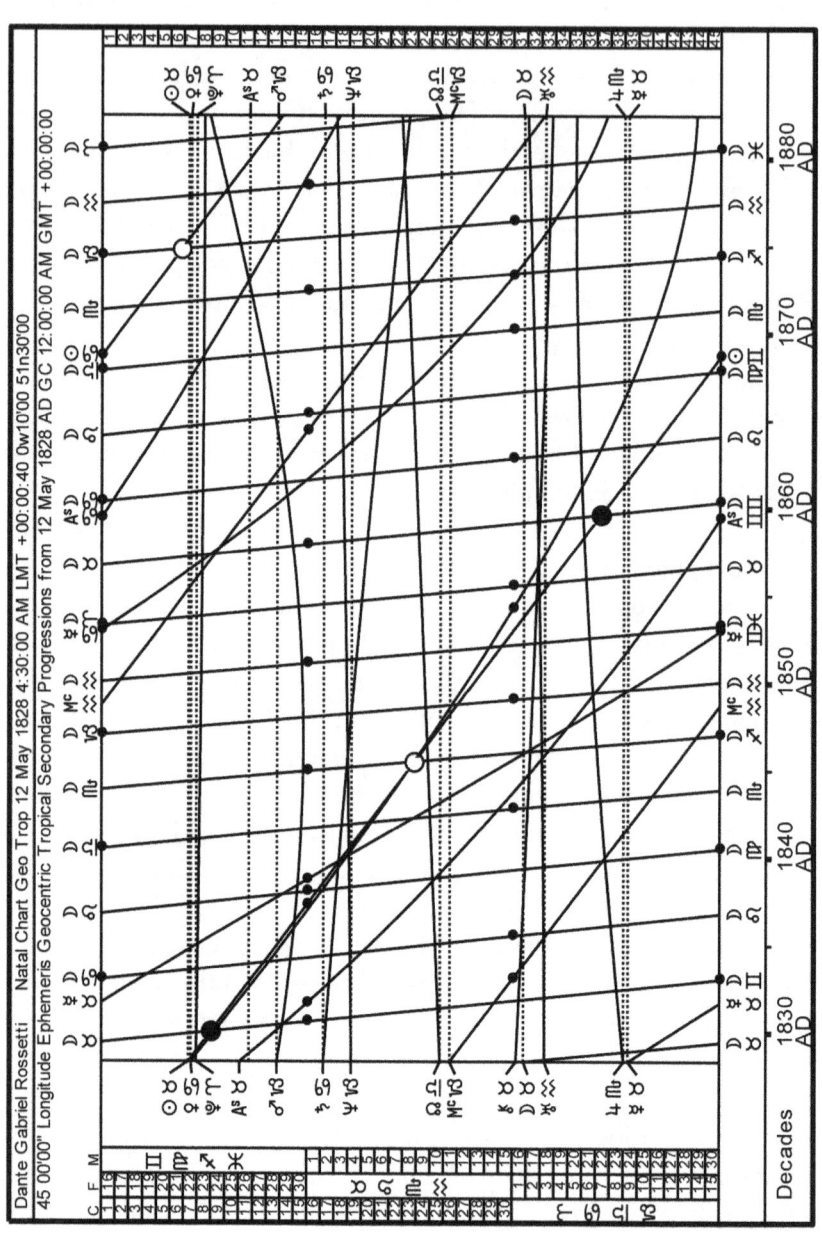

Rossetti – Lifetime Progressions

Symbolic Timing Techniques: Secondary Progressions 177

of Rossetti's planets and angles, starting with the Sun in Taurus, then Venus in Cancer, then Pluto in Aries. The birth position of each of these planets is drawn horizontally as a dotted line across the ephemeris. Following these lines from right to left and measuring them against the three columns on the left, you can see that the Sun is in the 22nd degree of Taurus, Venus is in the 7th degree of Cancer and Pluto is in the 7th degree of Aries. Because these three planets are clustered so closely together we know immediately that they are in a hard angular aspect relationship with each other. So we can see visually that the Sun (Taurus) is semi-square Venus (Cancer) and also semi-square Pluto (Aries). In other words, the Sun is on the midpoint between Venus and Pluto – an immensely significant piece of information in itself.

The birth position of the planets is also listed down the left-hand side of the ephemeris, and you can see how each planet gradually progresses across the chart.

Following the progressed Sun line, you can see that it crossed over the horizontal natal Ascendant line in 1834, when Rossetti was six years old, and over the natal Mars line in 1835, when he was seven years old. This tells us that his progressed Sun entered his first house when he was six, and made a sesqui-quadrate to natal Mars in Capricorn when he was seven. The following year, an exact progressed Sun-Mars sesquiquadrate formed, as the Sun crossed over the progressed Mars line. Staying with the development of the progressed Sun, you can see a dot on that line which corresponds to the year 1837, when Rossetti was nine years old. This is when his progressed Sun entered the next sign, which in this case is Gemini. With the progressed Sun now in the first house and changing to Gemini, we would expect a subtle but significant inner reorientation – a shift in the way he is going to express his basic creativity and relate to the world. Are you still with me at this point?

Audience: Yes, this is interesting. Go on.

Clare: The progressed Sun traces a more or less straight line through the ephemeris, since we know that it moves at a relatively constant rate of around 1 degree per year. You can see from the ephemeris that the progressed Sun remains in Gemini until 1869, when it reaches the bottom of the graph, when he was 41 years old. At this point Rosetti's

Sun progressed into Cancer, and appears again at the top of the graph. At the time of his death, the progressed Sun at 12° Cancer 57' is almost exactly opposing his natal Mars at 12° Capricorn 47' – within 10 seconds of exactitude.

Let's have a look at the Mars progressions, since they tell an interesting story. You can see that progressed Mars is moving slowly at the time of Rossetti's birth, since the line is very flat. Indeed, the graph shows us that progressed Mars never reaches the 16th degree of Capricorn, since it goes stationary in the 15th degree, where it remains for approximately eight years, from 1842 to 1850, before going retrograde. Mars is then retrograde for the rest of Rossetti's life, so his energy and direction turned inwards, applying gradually to the square with Pluto. He had a Mars-Pluto square when he was born, but by the time he died it had become exact by progression. So this is an example of an aspect which can take 54 years to tighten up and become exact.

Perhaps unusually, progressed Mercury never changes direction during Rossetti's life, but you can see that by the end of his life it is beginning to slow down. There are three planets retrograde by progression during Rossetti's entire life, Jupiter, Uranus – which gradually applies retrograde to square the natal Moon – and Neptune.

The progressed mean node gradually approaches square to Saturn, becoming exact during 1879, when Rossetti was 51 years old. With Saturn in Cancer, we can imagine how alone he was feeling, both existentially and emotionally.

Rossetti was born with Jupiter retrograde in Scorpio exactly opposite Mercury and Jupiter remains retrograde, moving only about three and a half degrees, and becoming stationary for the last decade or so of his life. A passionate, introverted Jupiter at birth, being both retrograde and in Scorpio, his journey to find meaning is increasingly inwards and downwards and backwards, so he is exploring the depths his whole life.

Neptune moves back very slowly upwards about a degree by progression during his entire lifetime. The same is true of Pluto – almost on the same degree for his whole life, although in that case it is moving forwards because it is direct. Saturn moves slowly, about five degrees his entire lifetime, and crossed Neptune – an opposition – when he was 22.

So I hope you will agree that this is a very useful technique if you want to watch the natal chart pattern gradually shifting, or to see at a

Symbolic Timing Techniques: Secondary Progressions 179

glance if and when any of the planets changes direction. Or you can just scan down your printed ephemeris, looking for a change of direction, which is an equally good way of doing it. Working on this level it is much more about inner process – realising what is unfolding from the natal, and not really focusing on events – but equally important because it reveals the shifting inner landscape.

Audience: That's the thing, isn't it? You don't get any clues from the outside world.

Clare: Isn't it amazing that astrologers are able to understand what is going on deep within an individual, and understand something about their inner development? This can help us validate our clients' feelings, even though there is nothing going on in the outside world to reflect that. So the more we can disengage from any kind of event based interpretation the more helpful we can be to our client – it's about using a different kind of approach and language.

Audience: Is this graphic ephemeris standard in all software?

Clare: Yes – just set it for progressions rather than transits and for, say, a 75 year period from birth, and you will get the whole picture.

Audience: How does it feel when a retrograde planet goes direct and returns to where it was when you were born?

Clare: Well then it is like beginning again, but this time with more in-depth inner experience of the meaning of that planet, so it is more mature. Does anyone have an experience or opinion about that?

Audience: My Saturn was retrograde at birth and then turned direct. When it passed back over its natal place it felt like the chains had been loosened.

Clare: Good. I do hope you all have some pointers now about the interpretation of progressions, as opposed to transits.

LESSON 10

Directions

Solar arc directions are of immense interest and practical use, so I hope you will build this technique into your future astrological work.

With progressions we are still using the actual movement of the planets and angles – but slowed down so that a day of clock time is equal to a year of our lives. With directions, we move a step further into symbolic thinking and add the same measure to all planets and angles, irrespective of their speed or direction at birth.

If we are used to working with progressions, this feels a bit strange to start with. For example, Pluto will move exactly the same distance as the Moon. So there is much more movement with Pluto and the outer planets, which now move approximately one degree every year, and at the same time there is much less movement with the Moon, which also now moves approximately one degree every year. But this makes the position of the directed Moon much more significant, because it is on the same degree for a whole year, and not just a month.

There are several different ways of directing a chart and it is worth knowing about the differences so that you can make an informed choice about which method you want to use for your own work. Your computer programme will give you the option of several different methods of directing a horoscope, and of course there is no single 'right' method: each one has its merits and seems to work on its own terms. It is certainly worth experimenting with more than one system, at least to begin with. One degree directions and solar arc directions are very similar and are the most commonly used.

Audience: What is the difference between these two techniques?

Clare: One degree directions are self explanatory and very simple, with every planet and angle in the chart being moved forward by one degree for each year of life. This is an approximation of the distance moved by the Sun in a day, and is a useful rule of thumb when we are looking at charts because we can easily add one degree to every planet and angle to see how far it has travelled in the same number of years, and we don't need an ephemeris or any software to do that. So that means that if you want to find your directed chart at the age of 15, then you would move everything on your birth chart forward 15 degrees. This will include Pluto, Neptune, Chiron, the angles, nodes and retrograde planets – everything.

Solar arc directions, however, are based on the actual speed of the Sun – or solar arc – in a day, and this is the technique we are going to be looking at.[1] And this varies, because the Sun moves slightly less than one degree each day in the summer, when it is furthest from the earth, and slightly more than one degree each day in the winter, when it is closest to the Earth. And this makes a cumulative difference. So for example, if you were born in the summer and you are now 50 years old, the Sun and all the other planets may well have only moved about 48 degrees by solar arc. And if you were born in the winter and you are now 50 years old, the Sun and all the other planets may have moved about 52 degrees by solar arc. The difference increases as we get older and can gradually amount to several years, which will obviously affect the timing of our interpretations.

Audience: What is the difference in interpretation between progressions and directions?

Clare: The core unit of measurement in these two systems provides some clues. With progressions, the Moon and its cycles are the main focus of attention. And of course the Moon describes our feelings and our ever shifting emotional landscape, which gradually changes the inner shape of our natal chart. So progressions are not generally concerned with outer events.

Directions are based on the movement of the Sun, and therefore describe the focus of awareness as the directed planets and angles highlight degrees in our horoscopes. Directions are only relevant in relation to the birth chart, since the shape of the natal chart does not change.

We really need to consider both progressions and directions, since Sun and Moon are of equal significance. As Liz Greene writes: "The subtleties of secondaries reflect the subtleties of the individual's inner 'weather', while solar arcs are much starker in their inexorable triggering of the birth chart."[2]

Directions tend to manifest, and can usually be linked to actual events because the Sun represents consciousness. But they do not seem to respond to a psychological approach, rather they tend to describe actual circumstances which are inexorably working themselves out, which is why they often feel like fate.

So, to summarise where we have got to so far. Transits are the easiest and most recognisable of the forecasting techniques, describing our response to events occurring in the outside world. Secondary progressions are more lunar, more internal and subtle in their influences, describing our shifting 'inner climate', rather than specific events, while solar arc directions tend to be more impersonal, being generally better indicators of events than secondary progressions.

Audience: I can't understand the reasoning here. How can we get our heads around this?

Clare: Well, all these techniques have gradually been added to our astrological lore over time. I have not read anything about the philosophical underpinnings of solar arc directions, but perhaps one way of understanding them is to go back to our time/space tube. The chart remains the same shape, but it is as if it was gradually turning as it ratchets up the spiral column at the same rate as the Sun.

Audience: OK, that makes some sense to me, like a sort of clock mechanism turned by cog wheels?

Clare: That's right. And the directed chart is only ever used in relation to the natal chart, which means that when we reach the age of 45, our entire directed chart and angles will be in semi-square to our natal chart. Equally, when we reach the age of 60, our entire directed chart and angles will be in sextile to our natal chart.

Audience: I have just had someone helping me to rectify my chart since I have Saturn around my Ascendant in Taurus. He asked me if I had had breathing difficulties or glandular problems when I was 18 months old, and I said no. But I was wrong, because in the end I phoned my sister and she told me I had mumps at that age and ended up in hospital.

Clare: So now you can be more certain about your actual birth time. Directions are an excellent tool for chart rectification because they so often point to actual events. Using your example, it seems that Saturn is 1½ degrees after your Ascendant, since that equates to 1½ years or 18 months. At this age, the difference between one degree directions and solar arc directions will be hardly noticeable. We can do very precise work with directions and refine the timing even more, since if we divide the year up into 12 months, directions will move at about 5 minutes of arc per month. This is why they are such a useful tool for chart rectification.

Let's have a look at some simple examples. Does anyone have an Ascendant right at the end of a sign? Counting one degree for a year, it is fairly normal to find that the whole family moves house, country or into a completely different environment when the Ascendant changes sign. Does anything interesting come up?

Audience: I have 27° Libra on the Ascendant and for the first three years of my life I was living in a big house on three floors with my mother and grandmother. But when I was three my mother had to go to work to support us all and the house was split into two apartments and I can remember this vividly because my mother wasn't living with us any more. I moved with my grandmother into two tiny rooms at the top of the house and my mother had her own apartment. This was a clear shift for me and I can remember these new walls because they made it impossible to go from one apartment to the other.

Clare: So your environment shifted from the comfortable surroundings described by your Libra Ascendant to the walls going up and your mother being hidden from you as your directed Ascendant moved into Scorpio. This shift in your environment, from Libra to Scorpio was built into your natal chart, presumably before there was any idea of the house being split, but it was already an event waiting to happen, which is why directions can seem so fated.

Audience: I hadn't thought about it in this way before. Is the Ascendant always about changing our environment?

Clare: Well, the Ascendant describes our personal interface with the outside world, on a day to day level. And the same is true when the Midheaven, and therefore the IC, changes sign by direction, which would normally indicate a noticeable and rather concrete shift in your life path.

Audience: What if you have 29 degrees of a sign rising?

Clare: Well, the first question is whether the birth time is accurate or not. This can be a real problem with English births, since the times are not officially recorded in the birth records. But if you are sure your birth time is accurate, and if we use the solar arc directed Ascendant, then it is likely that the whole family moved when you were one year old into a completely new environment.

Audience: Do you mean a physical move?

Clare: Yes, and in fact this is a very useful way of checking if the birth time is accurate. If your family had moved house or even country six months before you were born, then we might start wondering if your Ascendant was, in fact, half a degree into the next sign. I can use my own chart to illustrate this. My Ascendant is 1°30' Aries, and 18 months before I was born my parents left England by ship for Africa, and ended up in Zimbabwe. My early Aries Ascendant is an expression of the pioneering nature of the completely new life they had embarked on 18 months before I was born.

Audience: My family moved when I was five, but I have 21 degrees Taurus rising. I always thought my time of birth was accurate, but does that mean that my Ascendant should be 25 degrees Taurus, which is 5 degrees before Gemini?

Clare: It would certainly be worth experimenting with 25 degree Taurus Ascendant chart, and watching the transits, although I appreciate that this can feel very destabilising for a Taurus Ascendant person. New aspects to this Ascendant should give you further information about your actual birth.

Audience (Hilary): I am 60 now and by solar arc direction all the planets and angles have moved forwards 62 degrees, a bit more than one degree a year because I was born in the winter. My natal Ascendant/Descendant axis is 17° Sagittarius/Gemini and I have just noticed that my directed Midheaven/IC axis is now at 20° Sagittarius/Gemini, so it would have crossed over my Ascendant/Descendant axis about three years ago.

Clare: So the first thing I would want to ask you is what happened three years ago?

Audience (Hilary): That was when my first husband, my children's father, moved back to England from the United States. He had cancer, and thought he was going to move back in with us all, but he died.

Clare: From my experience of working with directions, one of the most significant events is when one angle crosses another. You had this three years ago, but from what you are saying, this seems to have more to do with the directed IC reaching the natal Descendant – because this was about your ex-husband and the father of your children and about the past coming back to meet you.

Audience (Hilary): That's interesting because he was a Gemini Sun with his Sun on my Descendant. And as a result of his death I have now bought a house in France and all his old furniture is there.

Clare: So the IC, which is the point of the home, directed to his natal Sun on your Descendant, and you now have two homes, which is of course a Gemini phenomenon. With your directed Midheaven/IC in the first and seventh houses, we could say that the focus of your life now concerns your personal and business relationships.

Audience (Hilary): That's right. I have been running a property business which he originally set up, but which came to me as part of my maintenance so that I could provide for the children. I was looking for a way to extricate myself from it when he died.

Clare: Well that is your story, isn't it, with Saturn ruling your natal IC – responsibility for the family. But if three years ago your directed IC got to the Descendant, then four years ago it would have reached Uranus, which is just one degree before your Descendant, so you wanted out, before this happened, so that makes sense.

There are many good examples of the way that directions correspond with significant events in the lives of famous people in Noel Tyl's book *Solar Arcs: Astrology's Most Successful Predictive System*.³

Directions – Case Study

Let's go back to Rossetti and see how some of the directions worked out in his life.

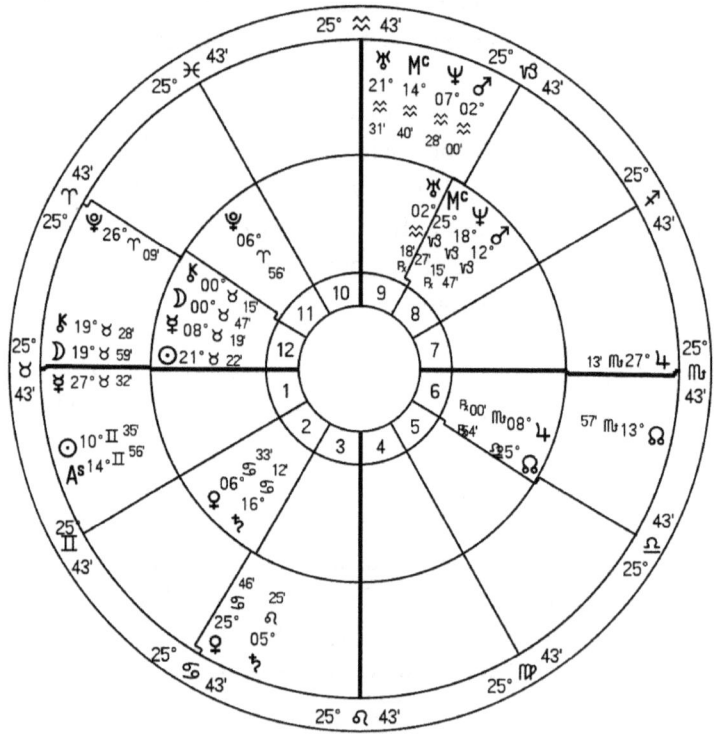

Solar Arc Directions on 12 May 1848, Rossetti's 20th birthday

You will remember that Rossetti founded the Pre-Raphaelite Brotherhood in 1848, when he was 20 years old. His intention was to restore art's connection to nature and to return to the abundant detail, intense colours and complex compositions of 14th century Italian and Flemish art. Above all, as an aspiring poet, Rossetti wished to develop the links between romantic poetry and art.

Venus, the planet of art and beauty, and of course the ruler of his Sun, Moon, Mercury and of his entire chart, has directed exactly to the IC at 25° Libra and is now squaring his nodal axis, on the pivotal point of changing values. Uranus has directed to square the Sun, so he has a new vision and radical new ideas. Simultaneously, Mars has directed to 2° Aquarius, onto his natal Uranus. Pluto has directed to 26° Aries, square his natal Midheaven/IC axis, which describes a total change of life direction. So you can see how remarkable these directions are and how they can even stand alone as a technique to describe the events of his life at the time.

And you might also be wondering what is going to happen approximately 18 months later, when the directed Moon will conjunct the natal Sun, symbolising a mystical marriage, and the directed Ascendant/Descendant axis directs onto the natal Mercury-Jupiter opposition. With the Sun-Moon conjunction, Mercury exactly on the directed Ascendant and Jupiter in Scorpio exactly on the directed Descendant, that is when Lizzie Siddal came into his life and became the living 'image of his soul'. With directed Venus on the IC we might even imagine that he had been waiting for his beloved all his life until that moment.

Moving on to the solar arc directions on his 31st birthday in 1859, Rossetti's progressed and directed Midheaven/IC axis is now in Aquarius/Leo, so he is expressing himself more freely, but there is tension indicated by the square of this axis to his natal Ascendant/Descendant axis, all at 25° of the fixed signs, and the directed nodal axis is now exactly on the natal Ascendant/Descendant axis, picking up all the angles, indicating conflict and tension between his goals and significant change in his relationships. This was the year when William Morris and Jane Burden were married. The Moon directs into Gemini and I would read this as the splitting of Rossetti's emotions into two, as a defence against having to feel the pain of the Chiron-Moon conjunction. Remember that Rossetti

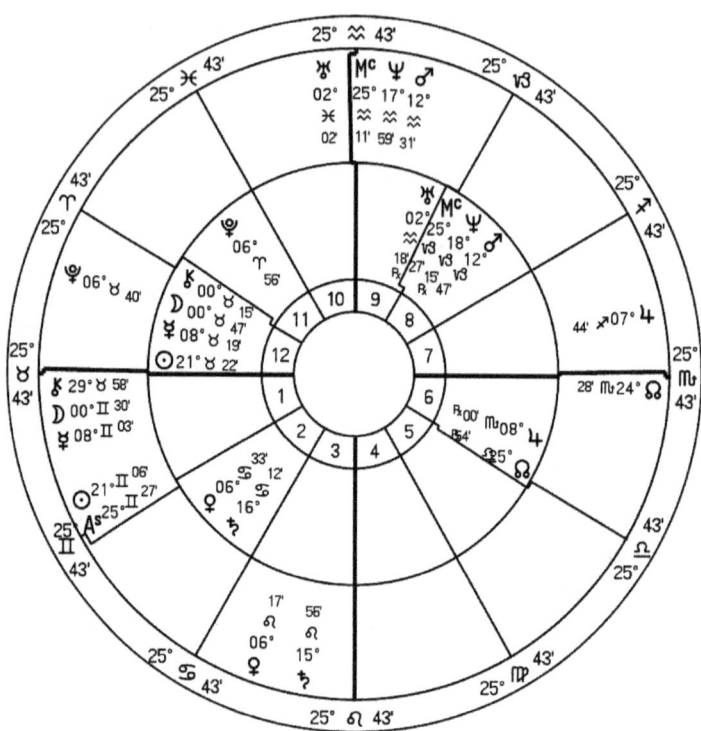

Solar Arc Directions on 12 May 1859, Rossetti's 31st birthday

is a strongly Taurean man with Jupiter in Scorpio. He needs to possess, to own the objects of his desire, to have and to hold.

As a matter of interest, transiting Saturn and progressed Venus are conjoined at 2° Leo, exactly opposite natal Uranus, so that is how we would use all these forecasting techniques at once, and it is remarkable how they tend to support each other, adding emphasis to the major themes. The Venus-Saturn conjunction can describe the end of a relationship, or disappointment in love, and we can also see the breaking off of a relationship when we add the Uranus opposition.

But the Saturn-Venus conjunction can also indicate marriage, commitment in love, and the following year he and Lizzie were married.

When Lizzie died in 1863, directed Pluto was now sitting on the Mercury-Jupiter opposition.

Venus is square that Mercury-Jupiter as well and the Chiron-Moon conjunction is trine the Uranus – so sudden separations. It's a double loss, isn't it? First his daughter and then his wife.

Rossetti became a virtual recluse after Lizzie's death but he started working with Jane Burden, who became his main model, and their relationship became stronger all the time.

Here are the directions for 1872, the year he had his breakdown. The main features here are the directed inconjuncts. Directed Jupiter is at 20° Sagittarius, inconjunct the Sun, Venus

Jane Burden posing as Isolde. William Morris

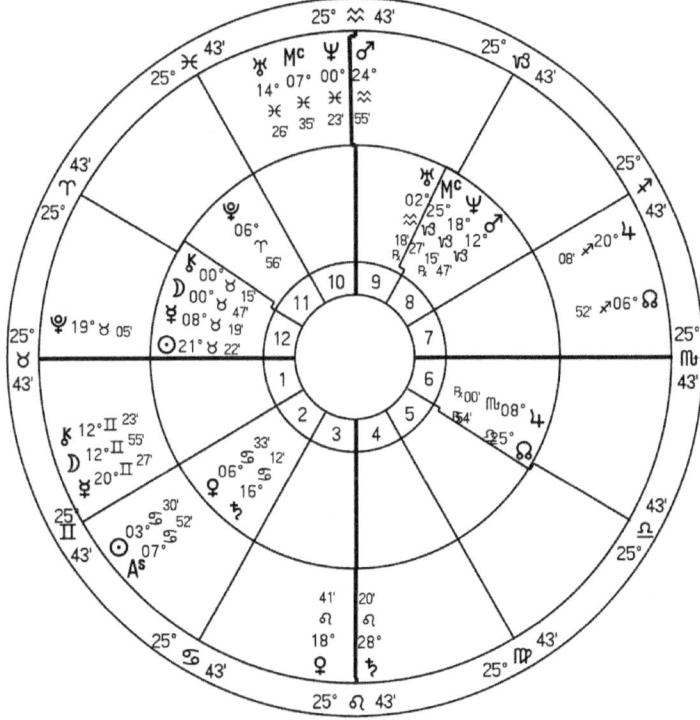

Solar Arc Directions on 12 May 1872, the year of Rossetti's breakdown

is inconjunct Neptune, which has just directed out of Aquarius and into Pisces, which coincides with his increasing dependence on drugs, the node is inconjunct Mercury, and the Moon and Chiron are inconjunct Mars. There is a great deal of stress in all these inconjunct aspects – they repeat again and again.

Directed Mars is now 25° Aquarius which is exactly square his Ascendant/Descendant axis and he was very sick indeed.

Here is another of his paintings of Jane, and here she is posing as an unhappy wife again – just for a change. She is modelling *La Pia de Tolomei*, from Dante Alighieri's poem in the *Divine Comedy*. Dante encounters La Pia during his travels through Purgatory, in Part II. She has died without absolution. Her husband was responsible for her death, imprisoning her in a castle, which is the scene in the painting, so that he

La Pia de Tolomei
Dante Gabriel Rossetti

could marry a countess. Rossetti always adds imagery to his paintings to help tell the tale. Rooks, which are omens of death, are flying in the sky. The sundial indicates that time is passing, and is reminiscent of the sundial in his painting Beata Beatrix, also a reminder of death. And most importantly, Jane (as La Pia) lightly fingers her wedding ring, the jewel given to her by the husband who trapped and imprisoned her.

Staying with the directions as our main focus, I want to show you the progressions, directions and transits at the time of Rossetti's death, so that you can see visually how all the forecasting techniques can be used together to create the whole picture.

The position of the secondary progressed Sun and solar arc Sun is always identical. In this case the progressed and solar arc angles are also identical, although generally the derived Ascendant is used for the progressed chart and the solar arc Ascendant is used for the directed chart, so the angles will gradually diverge.

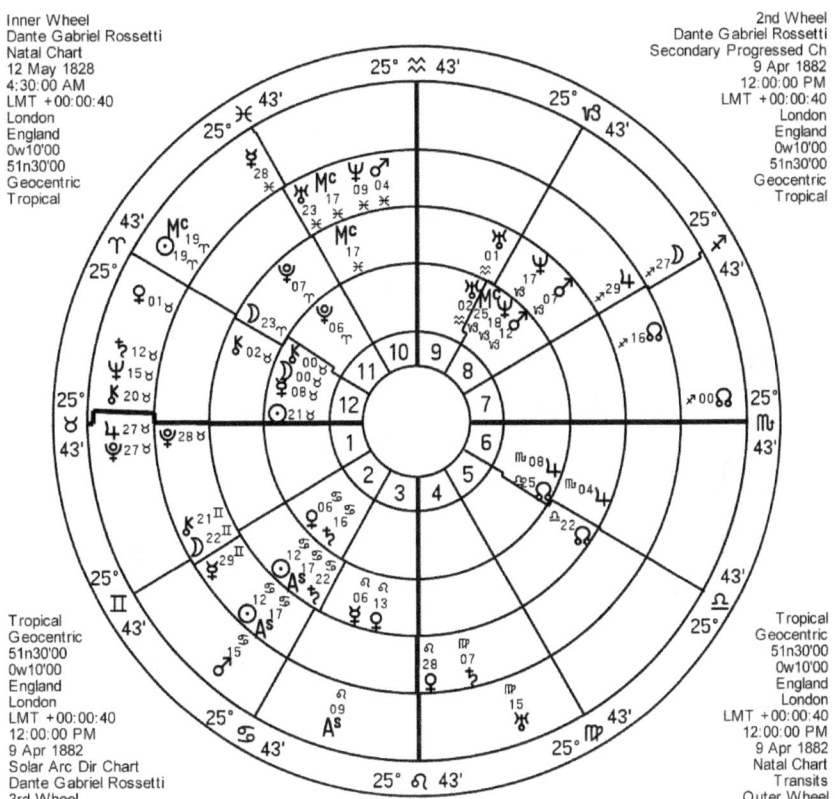

In this case, unusually, throughout Rossetti's life, both directed and transiting Pluto have been moving at the same rate – a reflection of the fact that Pluto moves very slowly through Taurus in its elliptical orbit. For those people born at the beginning of the 19th century with Pluto in Aries, Pluto would only have transited through about two or three signs in their lifetimes. And you can see that transiting Jupiter has recently crossed the natal Ascendant, has joined transiting Pluto, and is within one degree of directed Pluto.

Audience: But Jupiter protects, doesn't it? So surely that would protect him?

Clare: As always, we need to assess the meaning of Jupiter in Rossetti's natal chart, and you will remember that it is in Scorpio in the sixth house and retrograde. In fact, by progression, you will see that the orbs of the natal Jupiter-Chiron opposition square Uranus T-square have tightened up considerably from 8 degrees to 2 degrees, so this is not a particularly easy or joyful Jupiter. However, it certainly seems to be true that Jupiter transits do in fact coincide with death, which is worth thinking about, since Jupiter is the planet of long journeys.

Audience: Is it true that you shouldn't go on long journeys when Jupiter is retrograde, because you will encounter difficulties? I know that you shouldn't make any decisions when Mercury is retrograde, but is it the same with Jupiter?

Clare: Well, probably the best kind of travelling to do when Jupiter is retrograde is to go on a retreat, which is a journey within. Or perhaps to go on a pilgrimage or visit a sacred site, which would have a similar effect. Or to take the time to study something which is profoundly meaningful to you. But in Rossetti's case, with natal retrograde Jupiter in his sixth house in Scorpio, opposite Mercury, then it is also likely to be to do with health matters.

The directed Ascendant was conjunct natal Saturn the previous year, and Mars has now come to join them by transit. Remember that the Ascendant has been in the process of directing to Saturn since Rossetti was born. And the directed Sun is now exactly opposite Mars in the eighth house at 12° Capricorn, itself the focal point of the natal Mars, Mercury-Jupiter T-square. So Mars is triggering the natal Saturn as well as the directed Ascendant. Transiting Uranus is 1° from squaring the directed nodal axis, which is itself 1° from squaring the directed MC/IC axis. Transiting Moon in the eighth house is applying to a conjunction with the directed Jupiter opposite Mercury at 29° Sagittarius at 4.00pm on the day of his death, entering Capricorn two hours later at 6.00 pm.

CONCLUSION

Clare: Now that our course has come to an end, it would be interesting to hear your thoughts about what we have learned during the last year. For example, can you define what astrology teaches us which is more than psychology, philosophy, theology or science? What is the extra thing we are seeking which has brought us all here?

Audience: It somehow goes beyond everything else – and yet there is a tangible reality to it.

Audience: It provides an objective model that one can have a dialogue with.

Audience: For me the main difference between psychology and astrology, the special thing about the birth chart, is that it symbolises something very essential and original. The horoscope is a map with no moral or ethical judgements and no cultural overlays. We work from that very condensed map to see how it unfolds in each person, whereas psychology goes the opposite way, starting with events and going inwards from there.

Audience: There is something magical and mysterious about astrology which carries meaning and the message that people are not just mistakes, and I find that very reassuring. People are not just in trauma from their childhood or their potty training or anything like that. There is a bigger picture, and I find that extremely powerful.

Clare: I think you have hit on two very important points. Firstly that we are not just cogs in the social machine, which need to be fixed when they break down or cease to conform to the expectations or norms of our culture. And secondly that astrology lends dignity and meaning to what might otherwise feel like our own personal mess. It is a great discovery when we find that our own little life and its unfolding patterns are not just accidents, but a reflection of the entire cosmic organism. And I believe that this is why an astrological world view is fundamentally healing. Thomas Moore has this to say on the subject:

> "Through an astrological sensibility, we could learn that … life is not as fully subjective as modern social sciences would lead us to believe. We could sense for ourselves that we are indeed microcosms, small worlds sharing many of the characteristics of the immense macrocosm."[4]

Audience: I love astrology because it seems to provide food for the human imagination. We are dealing with a zodiac which we have projected imaginatively onto the cosmos and we are studying the relationship between that and ourselves.

Clare: Yes, and there are many different ways of understanding that relationship, all of which have their own validity. One way to understand astrology is as an empirical science which has developed over millennia of observation and reinforcement, studying the correspondences between celestial events and events on Earth or in the individual, in order to understand how the mechanism works, if you like, and I think that all of us are fascinated by that aspect of astrology.

Audience: It would be very limiting to approach astrology only from a scientific point of view. Astrology shows us there is something else as well.

Clare: I agree with you and I don't think anyone in the room would have any difficulty with that. Astrology also has a magical component and, when we embark on the ritual of studying a horoscope, with an attitude of enquiry and respect, I believe that we find ourselves engaging with a living tradition which can inform us if we are listening and put us into direct communication with the planetary gods. The point here is that the astrologer is inside the experiment – we are part of the organism we are studying.

Audience: Are you saying that we are actually transformed by the process?

Clare: Yes, and I am sure we all feel that when we study astrology. We become active participants, in constant dialogue with the living body of nature, in which everything is alive and interconnected, and of which we are part. We begin to live in an ensouled and enchanted world, and engaging with astrology is, in fact, an initiation into a new way of seeing the world and being in the world. As such, it should probably come with a public health warning, because our lives will never be the same again.

Astrology is intensely practical, and its beauty is that it is material – it works, as anyone who engages with astrology knows. The ritual of working on a chart restores our relationship to nature and brings us into alignment with the cosmos. Astrology cannot be explained, it only comes alive when it is truly experienced. And this is why we have to learn it with our whole being, and that takes time and a careful attention to detail, which is the purpose of our apprenticeship. If we are living magically we don't try to understand everything which is happening – we allow nature to remain mysterious. It can never be mastered because it is a living tradition.

Apollo is the god of rational truth, and rules knowledge, which is "to know about". His brother Hermes is the fertile god of the imagination, and rules gnosis, which is "to know from within". The world of the imagination acts upon us and has to be carefully protected from the clean sword of rational thinking. Hermes is the gatekeeper, standing on the threshold between different worlds, different realities and different truths, between consciousness and unconsciousness, between sleeping and waking. Gradually the magic and mystery of astrology begins to reveal itself to us.

> "An astrological attitude directs attention away from the self, with its subjective, conscious, and wilful decisions, toward an outer world that has its own mysterious ways of offering guidance and reflection. It gives us a concrete and explicit way to be in tune with nature, not just knowledgeable about it. Whether or not we practice astrology technically, it can show us a way to find deep guidance that transcends mere psychology. I would rather turn to astrology to expand psychology than reduce astrology to the psychological."[5]

Ultimately, astrology will always remain a mystery, which is defined as a reality which we cannot fully grasp intellectually, or for which we have no rational explanation. I would like to finish with another quote from Thomas Moore:

"With an astrological viewpoint, we can look beyond ourselves and into the world for signs of where to go and what to do. We can listen for suggestions from the world, of which we are a part, rather than initiating everything from subjective will and consciousness. This is the ethical dimension in enchanted living: deepening our sense of morality by learning the ways of nature. Astrology is in essence not a belief, a method, a science or pseudoscience, or even an art. At base it is a form of relationship between human life and the world, a relationship in which we learn about ourselves by observing the sky."[6]

Well, our course has now reached its end and I have thoroughly enjoyed working with you all on this wonderful year of discovery and wish you well on your continued astrological journeys.

Notes
1. Another technique is known as Naibod Arc Directions, in which all the planets except the Moon are moved forward at the rate of 59' 08", which is the Sun's mean daily motion, also known as the Naibod Arc. And for each year, the Moon is moved at the rate of 13° 11' – its mean daily motion.
2. Liz Greene, *The Horoscope in Manifestation*, Volume 9, CPA Press. Part Two: A Psychological Approach to Transits and Progressions.
3. Tyl, N. (1991) *Solar Arcs: Astrology's Most Successful Predictive System*, Llewellyn Publications.
4. Thomas Moore, (1996) *The Re-Enchantment of Everyday Life*, Harper Perennial, p.319.
5. Ibid, p.320.
6. Ibid, p.321.

Selected Bibliography

General

Campion, N.	(1994)	*The Great Year: Astrology, Millenarianism and History in the Western Tradition* (1994), Arkana, Penguin Books, London
Dethlefsen, Thorwald	(1984)	*The Challenge of Fate*, Coventure Ltd., Boston, Massachusetts
Heath, R.	(1999)	*Sun, Moon & Earth*, Wooden Books, Glastonbury
Hillman, J.	(1996)	*The Soul's Code: In Search of Character and Calling*, Bantam Books
Alice O. Howell	(1990)	*Jungian Synchronicity in Astrological Signs and Ages*, Quest Books, The Theosophical Publishing House
Jung, C.G.	(1979)	*Aion: Researches into the Phenomenology of the Self*, CW9, Part 2
Jung, C.G. (Ed.)	(1978)	*Man and his Symbols*, Picador, Pan Books
Lash, J.	(1999)	*Quest for the Zodiac: The Cosmic Code Beyond Astrology*, Thoth Publications
Ouspensky, P.D.	(1989)	*The Cosmology of Man's Possible Evolution. The Cosmological Lectures 1934-1940*, Agora Books
Mann, A.T.	(1984)	*Life Time Astrology*, Unwin Paperbacks, London
	(1986)	*The Divine Plot: Astrology, Reincarnation, Cosmology and History*, Allen & Unwin, London
Moore, T.	(1996)	*The Re-Enchantment of Everyday Life*, HarperPerennial
Jeremy Narby	(1998)	*The Cosmic Serpent: DNA and the Origins of Knowledge*, Phoenix, Orion Publishing Group
Sheldrake, R.	(2011)	*The Presence of the Past: Morphic Resonance and the Habits of Nature*, 2nd edition, Icon Books Ltd

Strachan, G.	(2005)	*The Bible's Hidden Cosmology*, Floris Books. First published as *Christ and the Cosmos* (1985), Labarum Publications Ltd.
Tarnas, R.	(2007)	*Cosmos and Psyche – Intimations of a New World Order*, Plume, US
Von Franz, M-L.	(1980)	*Alchemy: An Introduction to the Symbolism and the Psychology*, Inner City Books.
Whitmont, E.C.	(1969)	*The Symbolic Quest: Basic Concepts of Analytical Psychology*, C.G. Jung. Foundation for Analytical Psychology, Princeton University Press
Wilber, K.	(1996)	*A Brief History of Everything*, Gill & Macmillan Ltd.

Technical

Bell, L.	(2005)	*Cycles of Light: Exploring the Mysteries of Solar Returns*, CPA Press
Brady, B.	(1999)	*Predictive Astrology: The Eagle and the Lark* (Progressions, transits and the eclipse cycles) Red Wheel/Weiser
Clifford, F.	(2011)	*Solar Arc Directions*, Flare Publications
Davis, Martin	(2014)	*Astrolocality Astrology: A Guide to What it is and How to use it*, The Wessex Astrologer, Bournemouth (Revised edition)
Davis, Martin, ed.	(2008)	*From Here to There: An Astrologer's Guide to Astromapping*, The Wessex Astrologer
Dobyns, Z.P. & Pottenger, M.	(2011)	*Progressions, Directions and Rectification*, American Federation of Astrologers Inc.
	(1998)	*Unveiling Your Future: Progressions Made Easy*, ACS Publications Inc., US
Ebertin, R.	(1971)	*Transits: Forecasting Using 45 Degree Ephemeris*, American Federation of Astrologers Inc
Elliot, R.	(2008)	*Life Cycles: The Influence of Planetary Cycles on our Lives* Polair Publishing, 2nd Edition
Forrest, S.	(1989)	*Changing Sky – transits and progressions and the art of putting it all together*, ACS

Bibliography

Fortier Shea, M.	(1998)	*Planets in Solar Returns*, Twin Stars Unlimited; Revised edition
Greene, L.	(1986)	*Astrology of Fate*, Red Wheel/Weiser
	(1989)	*The Astrology of Fate*, Mandala, Unwin
	(2000)	*Astrological Neptune and the Quest for Redemption*, Red Wheel/Weiser
	(2001)	*Horoscope in Manifestation: Psychology and Prediction*, CPA Press
	(2005)	*The Outer Planets and their Cycles: The Astrology of the Collective*, CPA Press
	(2011)	*Saturn: A New Look at an Old Devil*, Red Wheel/Weiser, 35th Anniversary Edition
Hand, R.	(2002)	*Planets in Transit: Life Cycles for Living*, Whitford Press, US, 2nd Revised Edition
	(1975)	*Planets in Composite: Analyzing Human Relationships* (The Planet Series) Margaret E. Anderson (Ed.)
	(1977)	*Horoscope Symbols*, Schiffer Publishing Ltd (US)
Irving, K. & Lewis, J.	(2012)	*The Psychology of Astro*carto*graphy*, Words and Things
Lilly, W.	(2005)	*Christian Astrology*, Books 1 & 2, David R Roell (Ed)
Kirby, B. & Stubbs, J.	(2001)	*Interpreting Solar and Lunar Returns*, Capall Bann Publishing, 2nd edition
March & McEvers	(2010)	*The Only Way to Learn About Tomorrow* (Progressions, directions, transits, solar and lunar returns), Starcrafts Publishing
Meadows, D.	(1998)	*Where in the World with AstroCartoGraphy*, American Federation of Astrologers
Merriman, R.	(1988)	*Solar Return Book of Prediction*, Seek-It Pubs.
Michelsen, N.F.	(1990)	*Tables of Planetary Phenomena*, ACS
Rodden, L.	(1978)	*Modern Transits*, American Federation of Astrologers
Ruperti, A.	(1978)	*Cycles of Becoming, The Planetary Pattern of Growth*, CRCS Publications, California
Sasportas, H.	(2002)	*Direction and Destiny in the Birth Chart*, CPA Press, London

	(2007)	*The Gods of Change: Pain, Crisis and the Transits of Uranus, Neptune and Pluto*, The Wessex Astrologer
Sharman-Burke, J. & Greene, L.	(1997)	*The Astrologer, the Counsellor and the Priest*, CPA Press, London
Rudhyar, D.	(1967)	*The Lunation Cycle, a Key to Understanding of Personality*, Aurora Press, Inc. Santa Fe, New Mexico
Rudhyar, L.R. & D.,	(1980)	*Astrological Aspects, A Process Oriented Approach*, Aurora Press
Sullivan, E.	(1992)	*Retrograde Planets: Traversing the Inner Landscape*, Arkana Contemporary Astrology Series
	(2000)	*Saturn in Transit*, Red Wheel/Weiser, 2nd Revised edition
	(2005)	*The Astrology of Midlife and Aging*, Jeremy P. Tarcher
Tyl, N.	(1991)	*Solar Arcs: Astrology's Most Successful Predictive System*, Llewellyn Publications

About the Centre for Psychological Astrology

The Centre for Psychological Astrology was founded in 1983 by Dr Liz Greene and Howard Sasportas. Since its inception, the CPA has become world renowned for its unique and inspiring application of a variety of psychological approaches to astrology.

The Centre continues to foster the cross-fertilisation of the fields of astrology and depth, humanistic and transpersonal psychology. It hosts a unique seminar and webinar programme providing an original, informal and inspiring framework for both beginners and experienced astrologers. Past seminars are available as books and e-books through the CPA Press.

For further information about the current programme of seminars and webinars, to receive mailings and browse the CPA Press astrology books, contact the Administrator, Juliet Sharman-Burke at: juliet@cpalondon.com

The **Online Introductory Certificate Course** with John Green provides a foundation in the basics of psychological astrology. Run as real time online tutorials, students can interact with the tutor and other students, ask questions and watch recorded sessions.

For further information, contact John at: webmaster@cpalondon.com

About the Mercury Internet School of Psychological Astrology

The newly formed Mercury Internet School of Psychological Astrology (MISPA) offers a Diploma Course, and students who have completed the CPA's Foundation Course are eligible to enrol.

For further information visit: www.mercuryinternetschool.com or write to info@mercuryinternetschool.com

About the Faculty of Astrological Studies

The Faculty of Astrological Studies was founded in London to raise the standard of astrological education. The Faculty remains at the forefront of the serious teaching of astrology, preserving the links to this ancient craft, embracing new developments and passing on this knowledge to students all over the world.

Since its foundation in 1948, the Faculty has become known worldwide as a first class astrological school, and more than 10,000 students from over 90 countries have enrolled on its courses. Its Diploma is among the most highly valued and recognised international qualifications for the professional astrologer. Many of the world's leading astrologers are or were Faculty Diploma holders, such as Dr Liz Greene, Charles Harvey, Julia Parker, Melanie Reinhart and Howard Sasportas.

The Faculty's team of dedicated tutors, all of whom are themselves Faculty Diploma holders, are devoted to teaching astrology to students all over the world, guiding them carefully from the very beginning of their astrological studies right through to professional qualification at Diploma level. The Faculty's courses are comprehensive and flexible, available online and at classes and seminars in London. Full and part Diploma modules can also be studied at the Faculty's annual Oxford Summer School. Students can choose whichever method of learning suits them best, and alternate freely between them to suit their individual circumstances.

The Faculty's course material is unique, with a philosophical but practical approach to the art and craft of astrology, preserving its rich traditions and at the same time embracing and including modern psychological and post-psychological thinking. Course material is constantly updated, providing students with thorough, in-depth and comprehensive guidance, supported by their own personal tutor.

For further information visit: www.astrology.org.uk or write to: info@astrology.org.uk

Other Titles from The Wessex Astrologer
www.wessexastrologer.com

Martin Davis	Astrolocality Astrology From Here to There	Joseph Crane	Astrological Roots: The Hellenistic Legacy Between Fortune and Providence
Wanda Sellar	The Consultation Chart An Introduction to Medical Astrology Decumbiture	John Gadbury	The Nativity of the Late King Charles
		Komilla Sutton	The Essentials of Vedic Astrology The Lunar Nodes Personal Panchanga The Nakshatras
Geoffrey Cornelius	The Moment of Astrology		
Darrelyn Gunzburg	Life After Grief AstroGraphology: The Hidden Link between your Horoscope and your Handwriting	Anthony Louis	The Art of Forecasting using Solar Returns
		Lorna Green	Your Horoscope in Your Hands
Paul F. Newman	Declination: The Steps of the Sun Luna: The Book of the Moon	Reina James	All the Sun Goes Round
Jamie Macphail	Astrology and the Causes of War	Oscar Hofman	Classical Medical Astrology
Deborah Houlding	The Houses: Temples of the Sky	Bernadette Brady	Astrology, A Place in Chaos Star and Planet Combinations
Dorian Geiseler Greenbaum	Temperament: Astrology's Forgotten Key		
Howard Sasportas	The Gods of Change	Richard Idemon	The Magic Thread Through the Looking Glass
Patricia L. Walsh	Understanding Karmic Complexes	Nick Campion	The Book of World Horoscopes
M. Kelly Hunter	Living Lilith	Judy Hall	Patterns of the Past Karmic Connections Good Vibrations The Soulmate Myth The Book of Why Book of Psychic Development
Barbara Dunn	Horary Astrology Re-Examined		
Deva Green	Evolutionary Astrology		
Jeff Green	Pluto 1 Pluto 2 Essays on Evolutionary Astrology (ed. by Deva Green)		
		Neil D. Paris	Surfing your Solar Cycles
Dolores Ashcroft- Nowicki and Stephanie V. Norris	The Door Unlocked: An Astrological Insight into Initiation	Michele Finey	The Sacred Dance of Venus and Mars
		David Hamblin	The Spirit of Numbers
Martha Betz	The Betz Placidus Table of Houses	Dennis Elwell	Cosmic Loom
		Gillian Helfgott	The Insightful Turtle
Greg Bogart	Astrology and Meditation	Christina Rose	The Tapestry of Planetary Phases
Kim Farnell	Flirting with the Zodiac		
Henry Seltzer	The Tenth Planet	Bob Makransky	Planetary Strength Planetary Hours Planetary Combination
Ray Grasse	Under a Sacred Sky		
Martin Gansten	Primary Directions		

www.ingramcontent.com/pod-product-compliance
Lightning Source LLC
Chambersburg PA
CBHW070936180426
43192CB00039B/2287